Faith in the Future

FAITH IN THE FUTURE

by

RICHARD L. EVANS

from

"MUSIC AND THE SPOKEN WORD"

HARPER & ROW, PUBLISHERS
New York, Evanston, and London

FIRST EDITION

K-N

LIBRARY OF CONGRESS CATALOG CARD NUMBER: 63-21589

Contents

Marriage — "an Adventure in Happiness"

The Family Circle

Speech — It Hurts or Heals

Repentance, Improvement, and "Promise-Making To the Future"

Courage, Fear, and Faith

"There Is No Wealth but Life"

Foreword

"There is a future, O thank God!" [1]—a future of tangible hope and purpose and promise—and this book is dedicated to all who seek such assurance.

These pages have come from America's oldest continously presented nation-wide broadcast—"Music and the Spoken Word"—heard each Sunday on CBS.

Of this program and its participants *Life* Magazine has said:

Millions have heard them, and more millions, we hope, will hear them in the years to come. It is a national institution to be proud of, but what matters more is that Americans can be linked from ocean to ocean and year to year by the same brief respite from the world's week, and by a great chord of common thoughts on God and love and the everlasting things.

To you, the listeners, the readers, to all of you everywhere: We are grateful for your encouragement, and for your confidence in what seems to have become a common denominator, with the great and moving music of many faiths, many peoples, and brief restatements of the truths of all time—and for the great eternal principles and purposes that give solid substance to our faith in the future.

May peace be with you, this day—and always.

RICHARD L. EVANS

Salt Lake City, Utah
"From the Crossroads of the West"

Acknowledgments

Gratefully we acknowledge those who in one way or another have helped us continue on the air with the Tabernacle Choir and Organ for more than a third of a century—some for many years and some for shorter seasons. There are many, many more than these, but some we must mention:

President David O. McKay who has given constant encouragement; Chairman William S. Paley, Dr. Frank Stanton, and Arthur Hull Hayes of the Columbia Broadcasting System; Isaac M. Stewart and Theodore L. Cannon, President and Vice President, and Richard P. Condie, Alexander Schreiner, Frank W. Asper, Jay E. Welch, Mary Jack, and J. Russell Scott, all of the Tabernacle Choir; Geniel Robbins, exceedingly helpful secretary of more than nineteen years, and her associates, Beverly Harrison and Karen Yearsley; Marba C. Josephson; Arch L. Madsen, Joseph A. Kjar, Paul H. Evans, Richard A. Welch, Ray E. Loveless, of KSL; my brother David W. Evans; and Earl J. Glade, whose pioneering spirit and sincere community service were largely responsible for the beginning of this broadcast in July 1929.

To these above named and to others of a long and distinguished list—including the members of the Tabernacle Choir—our grateful appreciation.

Prologue

Have Faith in the Future . . .

"There is a Future, O thank God!"
—Henry de Lafayette Webster [1]

With so many opportunities and so many uncertainties, it seems appropriate to say to those who are searching and seeking—to those who are learning and preparing for life: Have faith in the future.

This is not only desirable, but absolutely essential to peace and progress, and to preparation. If there were no faith and no real reason for faith there would be no real point in preparation.

"There is no great future for any people whose faith has burned out," said Rufus Jones.[2] "Don't be a cynic," said Emerson, ". . . don't waste yourself in rejection." [3]

And in his essay *On Heroes* (written, however, for the ordinary man) Carlyle forcefully comments, "We have our mind given us, not that it may cavil and argue, but that it may see into something, give us clear belief and understanding about something, whereon we are then to proceed to act." It is a sad thing, he says, for a man or a people to fall

[11]

into skepticism or insincerity—"not to know a Sincerity when they see it . . . The world does exist; the world has truth in it, or it would not exist. A man lives by believing something; . . . a man who knows, as of old, that this world is a Truth, and no Plausibility and Falsity; that he himself is alive, . . . and that the world is alive. . . . Do not sink yourselves in boundless bottomless abysses of Doubt, of wretched God-forgetting Unbelief; . . . It lies there clear, for whosoever will take the spectacles off his eyes and honestly look, to know! . . . A man lives by believing something . . . " [4]

And so to the young—and to all others—we would say: Don't be discouraged; don't become cynical; don't be in too big a hurry. Be patient. The Creator is still in command. There are still principles—there are still cause and consequence; there are still opportunities, limitless progress to be made, truth to be discovered, peace to be achieved, solid purposes to be pursued.

Go on learning. Prepare as fully and purposefully as you can. Walk from day to day in willingness to work, and in a consistent, sincere living of life—with belief in its goodness and purpose, and with faith in the future. "The future belongs to those who prepare for it." [5]

* * *

"Go forth to meet the shadowy Future, without fear, and with a manly heart."

—Henry Wadsworth Longfellow [6]

[12]

Pressures, Patience, and Preparation

"A world where nothing is had for nothing."
—Arthur Hugh Clough [7]

How To Live with Uncertainty

How to live with uncertainty is an ever present problem—the uncertainties which suddenly change plans and prospects. Young men, for example, are sometimes suddenly taken away from pursuing life's preparation—for military service or other circumstances—and older men are taken from their families and professions, with much adjusting of their lives to altered plans and purposes.

This we would say to all who face such uncertainties: Go ahead with your life, your plans, your preparation, as fully as you can. Don't waste time by stopping before the interruptions have started. Keep going forward, and keep your hearts comforted, with courage and faith in the future. The world will always need the best-prepared people—and you must not needlessly hold back or slow down the pace of preparation that is necessary for fullest effectiveness. Don't quit or slow down sooner than is absolutely essential. The wise keep learning, keep preparing for life, and don't let uncertainties dissuade them from moving forward.

Even when interruptions come, whenever they come make the most of every time and opportunity.

Wherever you are, you take your thoughts with you, you take yourself with you. Wherever you are, you can think; you can read, you can study, you can learn. You can use the in-between times for profitable and constructive purposes.

In idleness it is all too easy to become cynical, to become careless, and to fall into questionable conduct, for evil always offers itself. So wherever you go, keep intent on solid plans and purposes. Don't succumb to uncertainty and don't feel sorry for yourself. No generation was ever sure it wouldn't be delayed or diverted from its plans and purposes. Few lives are lived without difficulties or disappointments.

Have faith, and justify the faith of others in you —the faith of loved ones and of others also—remembering wherever you are to be a gentleman, a man of honor. You take yourself with you, and you will want to be worthy to bring yourself back, and to be comfortable in good and beloved company.

Keep faith with the Lord God who gave you life. Keep close to Him in humble prayerfulness, in clean conduct, and your heart will find peace in all assignments and circumstances. Build for the future. Go forward in faith. Don't let any period become a blank in your program of progress. "Lift up your hearts. Be not afraid." Know that He *is*—and that He is mindful of you and will not leave you alone.

Speed—and Direction

In the long process of learning and preparing, young people often feel both pressure and impatience—sometimes so much so that delays or difficulties may cause them to quit, to give up too easily their pursuit of some good goal. Setbacks and uncertainties may cause a student to leave school too soon. Values may get out of focus because of problems or disappointments, and immediate things may seem more important than permanent purposes. In such situations there is danger of shortsighted decisions.

The unexpected almost always enters into life, and impatience must be tempered with enduring qualities of character and a farseeing sense of values. While it is good to go as far as we can and as fast as we can, as soon as we can, we need also to be willing to work and willing to wait, and should not too hastily set aside good plans for something secondary. "I have endeavored to impress upon the minds of youth," said Heber J. Grant, "the necessity of . . . working to the extent of their ability; and also while so laboring never to become disheartened." [8]

What if something solid and superior does take a little longer—even a lot longer! "There is more to life than increasing its speed," said Mahatma Gandhi.[9] Direction is more important than speed, and one of the worst things of all is to go fast in the wrong direction. We arrive at no good if we do not keep our course. Preparation is more important than speed. "The future," said Emerson, "belongs to those who prepare for it." [5]

"I have fought a good fight, I have finished my course, I have kept the faith" [10]—these words of Paul commend to us patience, perseverance, a reaching for perfection, and avoiding hasty, short-sighted decisions. "No life ever grows great," said Dr. Fosdick, "until it is focused, dedicated, and disciplined." [11]

You who are young: Keep your courage, keep your character and conviction; keep moving forward, and don't let passing circumstances easily discourage you from pursuing a good goal. In an age of speed, may God help us to keep clearly in mind the direction in which we are going, as well as the rate at which we go.

Pressures, Patience, and Preparation

It would be wonderful, in a way, if everyone could move directly toward his intended objective without delay or disappointment—without any slowing down or setback. But few have ever lived that way. And surely we would not develop much if everything were always easy.

We all have things to overcome. For most of us there are financial or personal problems—complex decisions to be made—decisions that pull us in more than one direction. Sometimes there are early responsibilities: marriage, family, other obligations.

Then, too, there are the ever present pressures: social pressures, status pressures, pressure to acquire things we cannot afford—things which would enslave us in debt and which, though highly desirable, are not really necessary—and when we begin to feel the burden of the price we must pay, we don't enjoy them as much as we thought we would. All values should be looked at with farseeing good sense, lest we enslave ourselves and let mere things become master of the man.

Unessentials can slow down the journey and greatly reduce our enjoyment. If we are carrying unnecessary equipment, unessential obligations, we cannot move so freely or easily either in preparation for life, or in the performance. We need to pace ourselves, to "run no faster" than we have "strength and means." There are some things for which we must be willing to wait, and not be short-sighted in settling for something second best or far inferior, when by willingness to work and wait we can arrive at greater competence and more of the lasting values of life.

It takes courage and character and common sense to avoid extravagant or unwise commitments, and to invest time and effort in preparation for the future. But the surpassing satisfaction of approaching our real potential is far more important than speed, and more important than insisting, right now, on something unessential.

The Pace . . . the Purpose . . . the Principles

Two essentials for a good and effective life are flexibility and firmness—flexibility in some things and an adamant and absolute immovability in others.

Frequently we hear it said that times have changed. Young people say it. Others do also. In some ways it is true. But it is a statement that can be seriously misleading. Many things *have* changed —some for the better, others with less happy results. There is much that is new in processing, in packaging, in promotion; in travel, in fashion; in tools and techniques. Almost every outward aspect of life has changed, and anyone who attempts to do business as it was once done would likely not long be in business. The pace of life has changed. We live in a faster and different world, both a worse and a better world, and in some ways we have to adjust to the times and be flexible enough to face the facts.

The pace has changed—yes. But not the purpose or the principles. Let no one be deceived about flexibility as to fundamental principles. We cannot afford to be flexible in matters of honesty. We cannot afford to be flexible in matters of virtue, old-fashioned as the word may seem. Flexibility must not mean setting aside considerate manners, or sound morals, or honorable obligations—or setting aside the commandments or tampering with the basic laws of life. We must discriminate as to changes and know where it is safe to be flexible and where it is imperative to be firmly fixed. To change the superstructure—the facing and the fashions—is one thing, but to tamper with the foundations is another.

The pace has changed, but the purpose and principles have not. The age-old, God-given rules of honesty, morality, responsibility—"commandments" if that's what we want to call them—and even the inner voice called conscience, are still what they always were, no matter how times have changed, no matter how modern we feel, no matter how flexible other things may be.

Unwillingness To Wait

There are many things in life for which we must be willing to wait. But too often, too young, there is too much tendency to try to rush life, to have it all now, to exhaust its experiences and force or seize things before their proper time and season —things both material and intangible. There is a tendency to crowd the future, to crowd the calendar and the clock, to forget not only eternity, and a reasonable future in this life, but sometimes—unhappily—even to forget tomorrow morning.

"In . . . modern society," said David Starr Jordan, "there is a tendency to precocious growth. . . . What is worth having must bide its time. Precocious fruit is not good fruit. . . . To guard his own future is the greatest duty of the young man. If all men lived in such fashion that remorse was unknown, the ills of society would mostly vanish. . . . The subtle incitement to vice . . . is shown in precocious knowledge, the loss of the bloom of youth, the quest for pleasures unearned because sought for out of time." [12]

Any premature harvest is likely to fall far short of expectation. Forced fruit, unripened fruit, is likely to be bitter. And it should be said that some fruit is bitter at any season—the fruit of indulgence, of unwise pursuits and practices that lead to dissipation, sorrow, loss of self-respect, and an unquiet conscience. As Robert Burns said in "Tam O' Shanter,"

> But pleasures are like poppies spread,
> You seize the flow'r, its bloom is shed;
> Or like the snow falls in the river,
> A moment white—then melts forever.[13]

There are some things for which we must be willing to wait. And there are some things that should never be indulged in. Some things are never worth the price paid. We need to take a long look at all values, all pleasures, all experiences. Nothing is deeply, lastingly desirable that is not earned, deserved—suitably acquired, and in its appropriate season.

On Knowing the Truth

Some centuries ago Nicholas Ling said, "Ignorance is a voluntary misfortune." [14] And John Locke later added, "A man may live long, and die at last in ignorance of many truths which his mind was capable of knowing." [15]

There are some things, surely, of which we are needlessly ignorant—and voluntary ignorance is a major misfortune. And as to acquiring constructive knowledge, we should have a continuing discontent and never become complacent or smugly satisfied with what we know of people, places, or principles. We should "study and learn, and become acquainted with all good books, and with languages, tongues, and people." [16] We should seek wisdom—understanding—and have minds open to truth whatever it is and wherever it is, since education is not only an opportunity but also an obligation.

It is sometimes said that what we don't know won't hurt us. This is as if to say that if a person has a disease and doesn't know it, it doesn't hurt him—or if we pay for good quality and receive shoddy or falsely labeled goods, it doesn't hurt us— or if we have lost something and don't know it, this is no real loss. Anything false or fraudulent, damaging or deceitful, has its ill effects whether we know it or not.

We need to know all we reasonably can—about physical facts, about people and their problems, about eternal principles. We should try always to turn light into dark places; to repent, to improve, to know more than we have known, to do better than we have done. We must seek to cast out fear, superstition, mistrust, misunderstanding; to penetrate the shadows with freedom to search, and with courage to face the facts—for "the glory of God is intelligence" [17] and avoidable ignorance is unbecoming to any one of us.

"And ye shall know the truth, and the truth shall make you free." [18]

Knowing Is Not Enough

When we are young we need to learn that we need to learn—that we need to know—that we need to acquire competence. Knowledge *is* power. It is a prerequisite to competence. "It is impossible for a man to be saved in ignorance." [19] "A man is saved no faster than he gets knowledge." [20] Goethe is credited with a striking comment. "Nothing," he said, "is more terrible than to see ignorance in action." [21]

These concepts are basic to the truth of all time. But in all this process of learning, in all our education and effort, we need also to know that simply knowing is not enough. There would seem to be ample evidence, for example, that Satan himself knows much, but uses his knowledge negatively.

Many, many things—facts, rules, laws, commandments, causes and consequences—have been known to man from the furthest dim past down to this very day—known centuries or ages since, but ignored. And new evidence and discoveries are constantly accumulating in matters pertaining to health, competence, peace, and a quiet conscience—evidences which, because of appetites or economic interests, are often ignored. It is known that many things are not good for man, that what a person eats, how he lives—his habits—have much to do with his health—yet appetite and habit often persuade people to act unwisely. Many things are known to be unwholesome for man, unwise to partake of, physically, mentally, or morally. Man has long known the commandments, the consequences of indulgence, of excess, of dishonesty, of falseness and infidelity. Yet many feel they can "play it smart" and somehow slip through—somehow be the exception; that they can set causes in motion without having to encounter the consequences. But in a day of much learning, of much knowing, of increasing knowledge, we still need to learn how unwise it is to ignore what we know—to learn that we must follow the laws of health and happiness if we would have health and happiness. Knowledge—truth—must be accepted, used, acted on, lived by. To know is essential; but simply knowing is not enough.

Commencement

There is an old proverb that says, "The journey of a thousand miles begins with one step." [22] This has many implications, but we cite it here to suggest that every period in life—indeed, every moment—is a point of beginning. With life, freedom, health, and the willingness to think, to work, to follow through, we have many reasons to be encouraged at Commencement. And to those who are both about to finish and about to begin—which includes us all—we would say: Despite all apprehensions and negative elements, it is doubtful that there ever was more opportunity, more open doors, or more genuine reward awaiting those who have courage, character, and the qualifications to take responsibility.

There are infinite needs—infinite things to discover, to develop, to conquer. Human wants are never satisfied—nor all the children ever taught, nor all processes improved to the point where they cannot be further improved. Full efficiency within our world has never been reached. The demand for fruitful ideas is insatiable. Dependability is always at a premium. Despite problems, fears, and uncertainties there is opportunity always for the person with knowledge, with willingness, with courage and character.

But the world is realistic. It does not give success to excuses—to reluctance—to laziness—to the dull or indifferent. Yet to those who will prepare, and then perform, the way is ever open. There are no known limits to learning or to achieving for those who are willing to continue with integrity and intelligence. Every day, every hour, every age in the life of man offers its own beginnings, its own opportunities. "The journey of a thousand miles begins with one step."

Faithful over a Few Things . . .

In the long process of preparation young people sometimes weary along the way. They become unduly impatient or discouraged, and give up, and settle for something less than the best they could be.

It is a trait of youth to be restless with routine—with the daily doing of what has to be done—to want to become what they want to become quickly, to want to start unrealistically near the top. But the pursuit of excellence is a long and patient process; there is no quick or easy way of acquiring knowledge, skills, judgment, quality—credentials. Competence and experience do not come quickly.

Even those who seem to have arrived usually spend much of their time in tedious routine, repetition, in the practice and performance of a daily round of duty. A violinist or pianist may be before his audience for only a relatively few minutes, and receive applause for only a few seconds. And for those few minutes of playing and those few seconds of applause there are uncounted hours of painstaking effort—of the drudgery of doing over and over again the practice that precedes performance.

Always there is the process of preparation—the learning, the doing, the willingness to work, the willingness to take responsibility, the willingness to follow through.

In the parable of the talents the Master said, "Thou hast been faithful over a few things, I will make thee ruler over many things." [23] We have to begin, we have to learn, we have to know; we have to do the lesser things before we can be trusted with the larger ones. This is a basic law of life.

There is much patience and preparation, much tedious repetition and routine, in the lives of all of us, and there is no short cut to excellence, to competence—or to the solid values of time or the limitless opportunities of eternity.

If "thou hast been faithful over a few things, I will make thee ruler over many."

Like Practicing in Public . . .

"Life is like playing a violin solo in public," said Baron Lytton, "and learning the instrument as one goes on." [24] We are often inclined to judge people by the flaws in their performance. We are likely to judge a young person, for instance, by some foolish or inexperienced act or utterance. People have sometimes carried through life the stigma of a single remark they have made, while hundreds of constructive, intelligent remarks are not remembered.

This does not mean that what a person says or does is not significant, or that he should not be accountable for his speech and actions. But there is no perfection in any of us, and in many ways people differ principally in the percentage, so to speak, of their goodness or faults.

To use another figure, the percentage of so-called perfect diamonds is very, very small, yet there are many beautiful stones that have some slight flaws. But we don't discard the diamond for the flaw. At this point, however, the figure fails us, for people are not static. They change. They learn—often they repent, often improve—and if a person's performance is unacceptable at some point, this is not to say that it may not later improve. While we cannot set aside the laws of cause and effect or suspend the penalties of a poor performance, we must remember that people change and move—they can repent, and they can improve.

The violinist whose music performance we pay to hear performs for us only after going through a long, arduous preparation, with many imperfect notes and unpleasant sounds and with much faulty fingering. But this is usually without an audience, while much of our practice in learning how to live is out in the open. Life *is* for learning, for practicing and improving, and it is not always easy, as everyone knows. We all need understanding—especially the young—for so often we do our practicing in public.

* * *

"In three words, I can sum up everything I've learned about life: It goes on . . ."

—Robert Frost [25]

"Only Let Me Make My Life Simple and Straight"

". . . A good conscience never costs as much as it is worth."

J.-A. Petit-Senn [26]

"Only Let Me Make My Life Simple and Straight"

"There is no true liberty nor real joy," said Thomas à Kempis, "save in the fear of God with a good conscience." [27]

The search of life is a search for happiness, for truth, for love, for understanding; for the meaning of the universe, and for knowledge of Him who is the Father of us all, who made us in His image, and who keeps all creation in its course. And in this search Rabindranath Tagore said, "Only let me make my life simple and straight." [28]

Ill health, heartaches, and unhappiness often come from searching for the right thing in the wrong way. "We degrade life by our follies and vices," said Christian Bovee, "and then complain that the unhappiness which is only their accompaniment is inherent in the constitution of things." [29]

"Mistake not those pleasures," said Jeremy Taylor, ". . . that trouble the quiet and tranquility of thy life." [30]

"The secret of all success is to know how to deny yourself," said Roswell Hitchcock. "Prove that you can control yourself, and you are an educated man; and without this all other education is good for nothing. . . . Every step of our progress toward success is a sacrifice." [31]

To all this Robert Louis Stevenson added that we should develop "the habit of being happy." [32]

Who would know better what will make us happy than a loving Father whose children we all are, and who has given us kindly counsel which we call commandments—counsel that comes from infinite wisdom, from one who knows our nature and wants us to have happiness and peace and the limitless possibilities of everlasting life.

"The habit of being happy" suggests a sincere seeking to know more of life's purpose, and the pursuit of it, with faith to follow a loving Father's counsel and to keep His commandments."

"Only let me make my life simple and straight."

The Obligation To Find Happiness

"There is an evident effort in nature to be happy," says a source of more than sixty years ago. "Everything blossoms to express beauty, as well as lead to fruitage. Even the inorganic fashions itself into crystals, that absorb and flash back the sunlight. . . . If one examines nature with the microscope . . . or considers the heavens at night, he finds three things: truth as inherent, beauty beyond that which can be spoken, and goodness everywhere. . . . God," says this observer, "speaks through all things, with an eternal desire to create happiness. Man has no right to be an exception—the only pessimist in the universe. The deep distress of the world comes in when we lose our anchorage of faith in Him." [33]

This thought, that "there is an evident effort in nature to be happy," and that the Creator "speaks through all things with an eternal desire to create happiness" [34] leads to this basic concept from another source: ". . . men are, that they might have joy." [35]

Much has been said of the right to search for happiness, the right to pursue it. But further than this, we would say that man has not only the right to search for and pursue happiness but also an obligation to find it. To be happy is indeed a duty. To this end man was made. And happiness cannot be found by running contrary to law, contrary to conscience, contrary to keeping the commandments.

What would a loving Father plan for His children—for those He has made in His own image—but their happiness, and peace, and growth, and everlasting life? And what he asks of us is to learn and to live in such a way as to be more like Him.

"There is an evident effort in nature to be happy" —and it should be so in men. The Creator "speaks through all things, with an eternal desire to create happiness." And it comes by living the Gospel God has given.

" . . . Cheerfulness and Constancy . . . "

Sir Richard Steele, eminent English essayist of the eighteenth century, made some whimsical and earnest observations on getting along with people, despite annoyance and inconvenience. Cheerfulness and constancy were emphasized among the qualities of character required.

"Some Years since," he said, "I was engaged with a Coach full of Friends to take a Journey as far as *Land's End*. We were very well pleased with one another the first Day, every one endeavoring to recommend himself by his good Humour . . . [But] this . . . did not last long; one of our Party was sowred the very first Evening by a [trivial incident] which spoiled his Temper to such a Degree, that he continued [to] Fret to the End of our Journey. A second fell off from his good Humour the next Morning, for no other Reason that I could imagine, but because I chanced to step into the Coach before him, and place myself on the shady Side. This however was but my own private Guess, for he did not mention a Word of it, nor indeed of any Thing else, for three Days following. . . . There were three of us who still held up our Heads, and did all we could to make our Journey agreeable; but to my Shame . . . I was taken with an unaccountable Fit of Sullenness, that hung upon me for above three-score Miles; whether it were for want of respect, or from an accidental Tread upon my Foot, or from a foolish Maid's calling me *The old Gentleman,* I cannot tell. In short, there was but one who kept his good Humour to the *Land's End.* . . . When I reflect upon this Journey, I often fancy it to be a Picture of Human Life, in respect to the several Friendships, Contracts, and Alliances, that are made and dissolved in the several Periods of it. . . . I must confess, there is something in the Changeableness and Inconstancy of Human Nature, that very often dejects and terrifies me. . . . [And] while I find this Principle in me, how can I assure myself that I shall always be true to my God, my Friend, or my-self? . . . Cheerfulness and Constancy . . . joined with Innocence, will make Beauty attractive, Knowledge delightful, and Wit good natured [and] will lighten sickness, Poverty, and Affliction. . . . In short, without Constancy there is neither Love, Friendship, or Virtue in the World." [36]

On Justifying Our Faults

The frequent human failing of pointing to the faults and defects of others in justifying our own is sharply questioned by Thomas à Kempis: "What is it to you if a man is such and such," he says, "if another does or says this or that? You will not have to answer for others, but you will have to give an account of yourself." [27]

There is a universal human tendency to look at what others do, to listen to what others say, and to take comfort in the weaknesses of others as an excuse for our own.

We are often disposed to say, "He did it," or someone else did it, or somebody's son did it—and so it is all right for us to do. In matters of dishonesty, immorality, cheating, or cutting corners we are too likely to justify ourselves by the errors and acts of others.

What everyone—or anyone—else is doing may be right or may be wrong—but the number involved does not make good of an evil act. The number of those who cheat does not make dishonesty honest. It is not good to follow a bad example, no matter how many others do.

On this point of dividing responsibility by multiplying the participants, Kipling gave us this terse, unforgettable sentence: "The sin they do by two and two they must pay for one by one." [37]

We all have influence with others, and anyone who does what he shouldn't do makes it easier for others to do what they shouldn't do. And instead of following others in a wrong direction we ought to lead them in a right direction.

We have an obligation to look at things as they are: as to their conformity with the commandments, as to their virtue or honor or honesty—and to look at ourselves and accept the right and responsibility of deciding for ourselves.

Beyond what we can see shortsightedly, we are sustained by the fact that the judgments of our Father in heaven will be fair, that He will not judge us by others, that we shall not receive more or less than we deserve, that no man will lose what he is entitled to.

We would well decide to follow good examples and not to follow bad ones, nor to seek to justify ourselves by the acts of others.

"The sin they do by two and two they must pay for one by one."

"You will not have to answer for others, but you will have to give an account of yourself."

The Quest for Unearned Happiness

It is sixty-odd years since David Starr Jordan made some searching remarks on a pressingly important subject—the pursuit of happiness. His approach is suggested by the title of his talk: "The Quest for *Unearned* Happiness [italics ours]."

"So long as man is alive and free," he says, "he will, in one way or another, seek that which gives him pleasure. But . . . to seek is not necessarily to find. . . . The basis of happiness is abundance of life, and abundance of life is a real thing, that cannot be shamed or counterfeited."

And then he cites an inscription he had seen somewhere: " 'There is no pleasure in life equal to that of the conquest of a vicious habit.' . . . This is the lesson," he continues, "of a life of struggle against the temptation of self-indulgence. In general, the sinner is not the man who sets out . . . to be wicked. . . . The sinner is the man who cannot say no. For sin to become wickedness is a matter of slow transition. . . . It is because decay goes on step by step that bad men are not all bad, as good men are not wholly good. . . . [And] the motive of most forms of sin is . . . the desire to make a short cut to happiness. Temptation promises pleasure without the effort of earning it. This promise has never been fulfilled in all the history of all the ages. . . . Unearned pleasures are mere illusions. . . . They leave 'a dark brown taste'; . . . their recollection is 'different in the morning.' . . . But true happiness endures, and leaves no reaction of weakness and pain. . . ." [12]

One indispensable part of the pursuit of happiness is recognition of the fact that, as Emerson put it, "the world looks like . . . a mathematical equation, which, turn it how you will, balances itself." [38] It all adds up. Basically and ultimately there isn't anything unearned.

Surely it is proper to pursue happiness. Indeed, true happiness is the eternal quest, the ultimate end. "Men are, that they might have joy." [35] What else would a loving Father—any loving Father—want for his children but genuine and enduring happiness and peace and progress? But as with all other things there is a law, a formula for it, and unearned happiness—happiness without virtue, without integrity, without effort, without inward and outward excellence—nowhere appears to be possible. As an ancient prophet put it: "Wickedness never was happiness." [39] (Neither was indolence, or indifference.)

There is no pleasure in life equal to that of the conquest of a bad habit.

Unearned Pleasures

"The motive of most forms of sin is the desire to make a short cut to happiness. Temptation promises pleasure without the effort of earning it." [12]

With this observation, previously cited, David Starr Jordan suggests some supposed "short cuts"—including indolence—that people are tempted to take in an effort to "secure the pleasures of rest without the effort that justifies [it]."

He then mentions gambling, "the desire to get money without earning it." But more insidious, he says, "is the search for the unearned pleasures of love, without love's duties, or love's responsibilities. . . . Just as honest love is the most powerful influence for good that can enter into man's life, so is love's counterfeit the most disintegrating."

He further says that there is real meaning behind the conventions of society and that the man "who tries to lead a double life is either a neurotic freak or the prince of fools. . . . That society is so severe in its condemnation of the double life is an expression of the bitterness of its own experience. . . . The equal marriage demands equal purity of heart and equal chastity of intention. . . . 'Even the angels,' Emerson says, 'must respect the proprieties.'

[And] the basis of the proprieties . . . is that no man should shrink from the cost of what he desires. . . . To [partake] . . . of love, in pure selfishness, without an atom of altrusitic responsibility is . . . to poison . . . life. . . . The strongest forces of human life are not subjects for idle play. The real heart and soul of a man are measured by the truth he shows to woman." [12]

Another forthright source has this to say: "The one great truth . . . is . . . that what a man sows that shall he also reap. . . . No [one] can touch sin without defilement . . . whatever . . . the philosophic point of view. . . ." For everyone "there is still the ultimate choice between purity and impurity, between truth and falsehood, between life and death." [40]

"So long as a man is alive and free, he will, in one way or another, seek that which gives him pleasure," [12] or happiness, but it does not—cannot—come unearned, and the seeming short cuts simply are not what they seem.

Character and Self-Control

"Over the times thou hast no power. . . . Solely over one man . . . thou has quite absolute . . . power. Him redeem and make honest." [41]

These words from Carlyle put repentance and improvement, and indeed all the choices and decisions of life, right back where basically they belong: with each of us, inside ourselves. They face us with the fact that the direction of life comes down largely to a question of character, which, in essence, is a question of self-control.

It is true that there are adverse influences and examples—that pressures come to play upon us—that appetites and desires and inducements pull us in different directions—but out of all this we ourselves have to select, we have to decide.

"A thousand ills come in through the open door of unresisted temptation," said David Starr Jordan.[12] Out of all that is offered, a man has to choose, to make up his mind; and he who cannot differentiate or resolutely choose the right—or who lacks self-control—has no assuredly sound future, for he cannot be counted on to make sound decisions.

Men make foolish decisions, sometimes by being headstrong, sometimes by failing to ask or accept advice, sometimes by being too conceitedly sure of themselves. There is safety in seeking counsel, with honest humility, from sincere and wholesome sources, and seeking it also from the Highest Source with a prayerful approach to every problem. "Self-control," said Lydia Sigourney, "is prompted by humility. . . ." [42]

"Every temptation that is resisted," said John Fiske, "every noble aspiration that is encouraged, every sinful thought that is repressed, every bitter word that is withheld, adds its . . . impetus [to] that great movement which is [tending] toward a richer life and higher character." [43]

This recalls another seldom quoted observation: "Do you want to know the man against whom you have most reason to guard yourself? Your looking-glass will give you a very fair likeness of his face." [44]

"The secret of all success is to know how to deny yourself." [31]

The Fallacy of the Collective
Cloak

Too often we seem to try to hide under a collective cloak, to assume that an act or utterance in the name of a crowd or a group or an organization or institution is something for which no one is personally responsible. "We live," said E. H. Chapin, "too much in platoons; we march by sections; we do not live in our individuality enough; we are slaves to fashion in mind and heart. . . ." [45]

But with all collective deeds and words, there is still a personal responsibility. Things simply don't do themselves or decide themselves. This hiding under a collective cloak, this shrinking from personal responsibility, this fallacy of supposing that something done in the name of a group is after all quite different from an individual action, is one of the reasons why crowds and combinations of people can sometimes stray so far afield.

There is no such thing as a collective conscience. Conscience is within each of us. And there is no such thing as making a wrong right simply because more than one person participates, or because each one considers his part to be impersonal. For our votes, our acts, our speech, our influence, our encouragement—even for our indifference or silent consent—all of us have a share of responsibility.

"Each of us here," said Carlyle, "let the world go how it will . . . has he not a Life of his own to lead? . . . The world's being saved will not save us; nor the world's being lost destroy us. We should look to ourselves." [4]

"Sin with the multitude," said Tryon Edwards, "and your responsibility and guilt are as great and as truly personal, as if you alone had done the wrong." [46]

"It is a very serious duty, perhaps of all duties the most serious," said Nathaniel Emmons, "to look into one's own character and conduct, and accurately read one's own heart." [47]

" 'Tis greatly wise to talk with our own hearts, and ask them how we stand." [48]

There is no known way, in groups or organizations or institutions, or in society itself, to separate ourselves by a collective cloak from principles or from personal responsibility.

Debt—a Sort of Slavery

"My father taught me," said Anne Morrow Lindbergh, "that a bill is like a crying baby and has to be attended to at once." [49] To a conscientious person, unfulfilled obligations are always a cause for concern. One reason is that he who *owes* another does not altogether *own* himself or his future. Some of his time, his life, his substance, is not in honor his own so long as he owes anything to others.

One of the great lessons to be learned by those beginning life together—as well as those who have lived long—is that payment must follow promises; that good credit, the right to be trusted, is one of the most valuable assets of life; and that debts do not dissolve themselves.

In all honor, debts must be met, value for value; and what we cannot afford to pay for today is not necessarily easier to meet tomorrow. As a whimsical economist has commented: "Expenditure always rises to meet income." [50]

But it does not necessarily work the other way; income does not necessarily rise to meet expenditure. And it matters little how much we think we want something—if the debt incurred in getting it is a burden and embarrassment, the luster of it is soon lost. A past-due, unpaid, or unpayable debt is a sort of slavery.

We cannot always begin where others *are*—where perhaps they have arrived after long years of sacrifice and service. "Be content [not] to want things that are not of absolute necessity, rather than to run up the score," said Sir Matthew Hale. "Such a man pays, at the latter end, a third part more than the principal, and is in perpetual servitude to his creditors; lives uncomfortably; is necessitated to increase his debts to stop his creditors' mouths; and many times falls into desperate courses." [51]

"A mortgage casts a shadow on the sunniest field," said Robert G. Ingersoll.[52] And Emerson observed, "A man in debt is so far a slave." [53] Furthermore, "consolidating" debts does not pay them. It merely changes the time and place of payment.

Human wants are insatiable. Man is seldom satisfied. And restraining the desires that would lead us deeper into debt requires both self-control and not being too much troubled by the problem of comparison. We should look to what we owe, to what we have, to what we need, to what we can do, and seek ever to be solvent. A man can have little influence unless he is sound and solvent.

* * *

"There can be no freedom or beauty about a home life that depends on borrowing and debt."
—Henrik Ibsen [54]

Marriage—"an Adventure in Happiness"

"With death, marriage is one of life's two greatest adventures . . . I would keep it an adventure
—an adventure in happiness . . ."

—Frances Starr [55]

To Those Now Married or About To Be

The poets have long written of love, in lines often quoted and in songs often sung—songs whose sentiment has given a lift and loveliness to life. But such sentiment does not long endure unless there is behind it some real substance, and what the poets have portrayed would perish without the basic qualities of character: qualities that include kindness and consideration, the willingness to give and take, to adjust, to talk things out with gentle, open frankness—free from sarcasm, free from cruel, stinging criticism, and with a fair and forthright facing of facts.

Marriage requires patience, temperance, moderation. It demands faith and forbearance. It requires willingness to work, to wait, and to honor obligations. It requires also a special kind of respect: respect for self and for one another; respect for feelings and convictions; respect for sacred things, and a prayerful approach to problems. It would be difficult to imagine the loveliness of enduring love without real respect.

No marriage—no life—is free from problems. There are always adjustments to make, things to work out, need for understanding. But in this most important and complete commitment, which includes the closeness of two people and all their future, and the future of their family, marriage must be deep and everlastingly enduring. Permanence and compatibility are worth working for, worth living for; worth cultivating the essential qualities of character.

Thomas Carlyle has given some advice that can be shared with equal benefit by those newly married, those long married, and those who are about to be: "Courage," he said, "and be true to one another!" [56]

What a stirring, briefly stated standard—what a great source of safety! Respect, kindly frankness, patience, temperance, honor, encouragement—and surely not forgetting the need for unity of purpose and for common convictions. With these the language of the poets may live to have much meaning. Have faith and courage, and "be true to one another"—and avoid the scars, the senseless costly separations, the deep cruel hurts of the heart.

Some Requirements of Marriage

Love, as already indicated, is not likely to live unless it is sustained by solid substance, by some essential qualities of character, qualities that include courage—courage to face facts, to meet problems, to make and keep commitments; to wait, to serve, to sacrifice, to prepare and provide for the future.

The list of qualities includes courtesy and consideration, along with respect and a certain dignity; also temperance and moderation that has the judgment not to overdo anything; patience with people—with children, our own and others, and with each other and with circumstances and situations—even patience with ourselves; thoughtfulness, and both faith and faithfulness, alike in love and in loyalty; reasonableness and gentleness. Said one who was wise: "There is nothing so strong as gentleness, and there is nothing so gentle as real strength." [57]

Marriage requires the giving and keeping of confidences, the sharing of thoughts and feelings, unfailing respect and understanding, and a frank and gentle communication.

Marriage, along with life, requires humility. We all need it (since we all make mistakes): the humility to repent, the humility to forgive.

And marriage requires both flexibility and firmness—flexibility to give and take, and the firmness not to compromise principles, the firmness to meet and keep obligations, firmness in doing one's duty.

Marriage requires a wise and moderate sense of humor without which the ways of life can be heartbreakingly abrasive. And certainly it calls for common convictions, so that both partners will be pulling one way—not pulling apart.

Marriage requires all these and much more, and should not be rushed into too early, or lightly.

We would plead with young people to take counsel, to be thoughtful and farseeing, prayerful and patient, and not rush into a decision of such incalculable concern, of such everlasting consequence.

A Gentle, Kindly
Communication

A gentle, kindly, open communication is one of the essential qualities for the day-to-day understanding of each other and for explaining many moods and avoiding many hurts. There is sometimes need for silence and sometimes need for talk, and both have their place and purpose.

Moreover, there are different kinds of silence: there is thoughtful silence; peaceful, understanding silence; there is moody silence and inconsiderate silence. There is also hurt silence—the silence in which people harbor hurts in their hearts and brood about them, or imagine offenses, or make small things seem large in their own minds and fail to bring them out into the open.

Marriage is a sharing, a giving, of ourselves. And this means sharing and giving our thoughts, our minds, our moods, our hopes and dreams, our plans and purposes, in closest confidence. Those who are so closely associated and concerned, so closely and rightfully part of a partnership, need to know, to understand, to communicate and get through to each other. Small hurts, and large ones also, can often be avoided if there is understanding, and

[61]

there can be understanding only if there is communication.

This does not necessarily mean loquacious communication, nor only talking about big things. There is wisdom and satisfaction and closeness of confidence in sharing small things also—what happened during the day, the small successes, failures, hopes and feelings. And fears, too, may be softened by gentle, kindly communication.

In marriage there must be a completeness of confidence and a completeness of understanding also. These call for an open channel of communication, a two-way interchange of thoughts and feelings. Where things are harbored in the heart, with no adequate outlet, real or imagined, they may fester and build up pressure.

One of the essentials of safety and success in marriage is an open channel for quiet, confident, and kindly two-way talk—frank when it needs to be, and honest, but always gentle, always understanding, always kindly and considerate—a communication that is never cutting or unkind.

"Cheerfulness and Constancy" in Marriage

Here are some lines on a lasting marriage written by Sir Richard Steele in a two-hundred-and-fifty-year-old essay.

"The most delightful and most lasting Engagements," he said, "are generally those which pass between Man and Woman; and yet upon what Trifles are they weakened, or intirely broken?" Sometimes, he says, "the Parties fly asunder even in the Midst of Courtship, sometimes grow cool" in the early months of marriage, while "others continue good till thirty, others till forty, while some . . . whose Souls are of an happier Make . . . travel on together to the End of their Journey in . . . continual . . . kind Offices and mutual Endearments. When we therefore chuse our Companions for Life, if we hope to keep both them and ourselves in good Humour to the last stage of it, we must be extreamly careful in the Choice we make, as well as in the Conduct on our Part. When the Persons to whom we join ourselves can stand an Examination, and bear the Scrutiny, when they mend upon . . . Acquaintance . . . and [we] discover new Beauties the more we search"—then our love will naturally grow.

"But because there are very few possessed of such accomplishments of Body and Mind, we ought to look after those Qualifications both in ourselves and others, which are indispensably necessary towards this happy Union, and which are in the Power of every one to acquire, or at least to cultivate and improve. These, in my Opinion, are *Cheerfulness and Constancy* . . . [italics ours]"

These qualities, says Sir Richard, may be acquired even by those of greatest fickleness, "who consider seriously the Terms of Union upon which they come together, the mutual Interest in which they are engaged, with all the Motives that ought to incite their Tenderness and Compassion towards those who have . . . Dependence upon them, and are embarked with them for Life in . . . Happiness or Misery. Constancy becomes a moral Virtue . . . that is not subject to any Change of Health, Age, Fortune, or . . . Accidents. . . ." Where such a constancy is lacking, he concludes, the most ardent fondness "may fall away into coldness and Indifference." [36]

"To be content with even the best people," wrote Francis de S. Fenelon, "we must be contented with little and bear a great deal." For "even those who are most perfect have many imperfections, and we [all] have great faults." [58]

Perhaps any one of us could get along with perfect people. But our task is to get along with imperfect people, which is what all of us are, and for this we need the character and constancy that will survive the imperfections we all have.

What Is Love without Truth?

Back in the seventeenth century John Tillotson said, "It is hard to personate and act a part long; for where truth is not at the bottom nature will always be endeavoring to return, and will peep out and betray herself one time or another." [59]

"Hypocrisy is folly," wrote Richard Cecil. "It is much easier, safer, and pleasanter to be the thing which a man appears, than to keep up the appearance of what he is not." [60]

"God has given you one face," Shakespeare said, "and you make yourself another." [61]

From these generalizations let us consider one exceedingly important phase of the subject of sincerity, with a challenging quoted question: "What is love without truth?" [62]

This suggests the importance of frankness and fairness in sharing interests and activities; fairness and frankness in reporting things done and seen, in reporting as to places and people; frankness and fairness in family finances and in facing facts. It also suggests the question of deception, of infidelity, of alleging love, of leading a double life.

Marriage is such a basic, sacred, and vital relationship in life that it must be fixed on solid foundations and cannot safely be subjected to pretense, to double standards, divided loyalties, and deceit. Love is entitled to loyalty. Marriage cannot be truly happy, or safe, or solid, if there is a mere appearance of confidence and compatibility, of faith and faithfulness. For family solidarity and the sanctity of the home and of marriage there cannot safely be shaded areas; there cannot safely be deception.

To recall again the question, "What is love without truth?"—indeed, what is anything without truth?

Love Is All This . . .

Sincere love is something that sacrifices—not something that indulges itself. Sincere love is responsible. It would never knowingly hurt, but would heal.

"We are too ready to retaliate, rather than forgive. . . ." said William Penn, "And yet we could hurt no Man that we believe loves us. . . . What we love we'll trust. . . . Love," he continued, "is the hardest Lesson in Christianity. . . ." [63]

"Love is a great thing, a good above all others," said Thomas à Kempis, "which alone maketh every burden light. . . . Love is watchful, and whilst sleeping still keeps watch; though fatigued, it is not weary; though pressed, it is not forced. . . . Love is . . . sincere . . . gentle, strong, patient, faithful, prudent, long-suffering, manly. . . . Love is circumspect, humble, and upright; not weak, not fickle, nor intent on vain things; sober, chaste, steadfast, quiet, and guarded in all the senses." [27]

Love is doing, forgiving, serving, shielding, protecting, cherishing, respecting. It is not mere passing sentiment, but something solid that can be counted on. "If we lose affection and kindliness from our life," said Cicero, "we lose all that gives it charm." [64]

"This is the one remedy for all ills," observed Emerson. "We must [love], and at once the impossible becomes possible. . . . Let our affection flow out to our fellows; [and] it would operate in a day the greatest of all revolutions. . . . Love would put a new face on this weary . . . world." [65]

"Love and you shall be loved." [38]

"Thou shalt live together in love. . . ." [66]

This all adds up to a great scriptural injunction: "This is my commandment, That ye love one another, as I have loved you." [67] And to the question "What is love without truth?" one may almost equally ask, "What is truth without love?"

In short, love is not just something we say—for love seeks truth and requires honesty and honor, discipline and self-control. It is a very substance of soul that cannot be selfish. And merely saying that we love is not enough.

To "Live Together in Love"

If a man loves truth, he will live it; and to live truth requires self-control. "No man has a right to do as he pleases, except when he pleases to do right." [68]

"Men's hearts," said Carlyle, "ought not to be set against one another, but . . . against evil only." [41]

"More hearts pine away in secret anguish for unkindness from those who should be their comforters, than for any other calamity in life." [69]

"Each one of us is bound to make the . . . circle in which he lives better and happier." [70]

"What do we live for," asked George Eliot, "if it is not to make life less difficult to each other?" [71]

". . . if ye have known of . . . the goodness . . . of God," said King Benjamin, "and have tasted of his love . . . ye will not have a mind to injure one another, but to live peaceably, and to render to every man according to that which is his due. And ye will not suffer your children . . . that they transgress the laws of God, and fight and quarrel one with another. . . . But ye will teach them to walk in the ways of truth and soberness; ye will teach them to love one another, and to serve one another. And also, ye yourselves will succor those that stand in need . . . ye will administer of your substance unto him that standeth in need. . . ." [72]

We turn again to the sentence from William Penn—that "love is the hardest Lesson in Christianity." [63] It may be the hardest lesson in life, yet surely it is one of the most essential. "Love or perish" [73] are the alternatives offered.

And love must have truth if it is to last, and along with truth comes law, and the living of law requires self-control, and self-control requires character, without which there is nothing we can count on.

In the spirit of Him who offered His love, and who gave His life that men might live, let us "live together in love" [66]—with truth and character and kindliness, in the spirit of the Prince of Peace. "No man has a right to do as he pleases, except when he pleases to do right."

Repentance—and the Failure to Forgive

In one of his writings, previously cited, India's Tagore said, "Only let me make my life simple and straight." [28] But this we do not always do. We let life become cluttered and complicated.

We make mistakes, for which we need repentance and forgiveness. And in needing forgiveness we must offer it to others also.

No one is as happy as he could be if he has a conflict with conscience or has not honestly repented of an unworthy act. Nor is anyone as happy as he could be if he is grudgingly withholding his forgiveness from a sincerely repentant person. "He that cannot forgive others," said George Herbert, "breaks the bridge over which he himself must pass . . . for every one has need to be forgiven." [74] All our lives would be unhappy and frustrated without the blessed principle and privilege of repentance, and well would we remember what the Master said concerning our obligation to forgive others as we would be forgiven.

If a truly repentant person were to approach another person sincerely and repeatedly, but always find an unrelenting, unforgiving attitude, there would come a time when the offender would feel that there was no use trying to make amends. Hopelessness, indifference, and a "don't care" attitude may result from an unreasonable, stubborn failure to forgive. And if we are obdurately unforgiving, if we are unreasonably unapproachable to the sincerely repentant person, we may take upon ourselves an added element of responsibility for future offense, since in the unreasonable failure to forgive we take away, in part, the reason for repenting.

The obligation works both ways—on the offended as well as the offender—on the one, to see that his repentance is sincere and not superficial—sincere to the point of changing his ways and trying to make amends—and on the other, to accept a sincere repentance.

We all make mistakes; we all need understanding; we all need repentance and forgiveness. "He that cannot forgive others, breaks the bridge over which he himself must pass. . . ."

Repentance and Sincerity

As to sincerity in repentance, simply saying the words—simply saying we are sorry—is not enough. The persistent repeating of former offenses suggests a certain lack of sincerity, or at least of self-control. "Prove that you can control yourself," said Roswell Dwight Hitchcock, "and you are an educated man; and without this all other education is good for nothing. . . ." [31]

Suppose someone who has injured or offended another comes to him and says, "I'm sorry," and because he says so we assume his regret is sincere. Then suppose the next day he does the same thing, and again says, "I'm sorry"—and keeps on doing the same thing and keeps on saying he is sorry. Surely there comes a point when one wonders how sincere he is in repenting and in repeatedly saying, "I'm sorry."

The limits of patience of the Judge and Father of us all, of course, we do not know; though we have reason to be thankful that His patience and love and understanding are very great. Yet is it wise to press that patience beyond a reasonable point, in persistent repeating of offenses, and in insincere repenting?

"By this ye may know if a man repenteth of his

sins—behold, he will confess them and forsake them." [75] This accords with the Master's words when he said: "Go, and sin no more." [76] Sometimes the latter part is underemphasized.

"Immorality in any society," says a current source, "is defined by the magnitude of the gap between ideals and behavior." [77] In other words, the difference, the gap, between what we say and what we do may be the measure of our sincerity, in repentance as in all else also.

"Profound sincerity," said Emerson, "is the only basis of talent as of character." [8] And it follows that, to be effective, repentance must be sincere.

* * *

"The sum which two married people owe to one another defies calculation. It is an infinite debt, which can only be discharged through all eternity."

—Goethe [78]

The Family Circle

"Do they miss me at home—do they miss me?
'Twould be an assurance most dear,
To know that this moment some loved one
Were saying, 'I wish he were here.' "
—Caroline Atherton Briggs Mason [79]

Domestic Diplomacy

In many places people are ingratiating as a matter of policy. Public relations, so-called, have come to be important to both individuals and organizations—that is, the impression—the "image"—with which we are, in other minds, inseparably associated. Merchants, manufacturers, professional men, and many others learn the importance of these impressions. All this is readily recognized in many relationships of life.

And it would seem that this should also be as readily recognized, or more so, at home, with those we love and live with in the closest of all associations—with those who mean the most.

Are not these who belong to us, and to whom we belong, entitled to see the better side of ourselves —not the most formal side, perhaps, but the most understanding and considerate side; to hear our thanks, to know of our interest, share our confidences; to give and take, and be accommodated even at our own inconvenience? Are they not entitled to see us groomed and pleasant and personable; to receive pleasant replies, and to know, and hear, and feel our gratitude and love and loyalty?

Sometimes it might be well to ask ourselves what it would be like not to be able to go home—not to have a place in the family circle—not to have a sense of belonging—not to know that there are some who share our sorrows and successes or who feel a personal responsibility, as if we were personally a part of them.

God has given us no greater blessing than that of belonging to a loving and loyal family, of having a home, a place where we are welcome and understood, free from fear of being unkindly quoted; a place where all our interests are sincerely considered and served. Surely such a place deserves the best of all we can give—deserves to see and hear the better side of ourselves, and to receive from us a fair share of service in all the thousand things it takes to keep it going. Home deserves our consideration, our appreciation, our help, and a faithful, pleasant performance on our part.

"God Bless Our Home" is a motto that once appeared on many walls. And He will bless it, and us, if we bless each other and serve and live and share in love and loyalty. Home is, or can be—should be —the nearest thing we have to a heaven on earth.

The Family Circle

What if each day as we awoke we were aware of being one day nearer the absolute and final end of all that means most to us—the end, forever, of seeing beloved faces of family and friends, the end of life's sweetest associations. If this, indeed, were our actual outlook, frustration and cynicism would be easy to understand, and life's most wonderful memories would be marred with a sharp and anguished sorrow. Indeed, what is most dearly loved and then wholly lost must be a matter of gnawing grief and regret.

But this, most blessedly, is not the pattern or purpose or promise that God has given. Yet suppose it were—suppose that even here and now we were to lose our place in the circle of family and friends; suppose that we could never again be with those who mean most to us; suppose that we could never again go home to loved ones waiting. Life would be cruel and empty under such circumstances.

George Eliot said, in a striking sentence: "I desire no future that will break the ties of the past." [71] The ties to life, to loved ones—to the blessed, everlasting reality of family and friends, to things that we can count on—give faith and peace and purpose and assurance for the future.

And so for those who have lost, or who may lose, those they most love, we come again to the reaffirming of this faith: faith in the eternal continuance of truth, intelligence, personality, and of personal eternal progress; faith in the literal reality of everlasting life with those we love.

In time, as in eternity, there is nothing more blessed or important than the completeness of the family circle and the place each of us has in it. And knowing many who have gone before, we may know how wonderful it must be where loved ones wait.

"I desire no future that will break the ties of the past"—for heaven could only be heaven with family and friends.

Those Whom God Has Given Us

There is a much-quoted phrase from Scripture about being our brother's keeper. But if it is important to be our brother's keeper, which we cannot doubt, how very important it must be to be our children's keeper—the keeper of our families, our loved ones, those whom God has given us.

Indeed, it would be difficult to deny that responsibility for our children is one of the greatest responsibilities God has given us. And while there may be much that parents cannot do for their children as well as others can, there is also much that others cannot do as appropriately as parents.

Parents may not be prepared to prescribe for children in some ailments and illnesses; parents may not be able to teach their children many technical subjects, or train them in the development of some of their talents. Yet there is a special calling, a special mission, a special responsibility that God has given parents in relation to their children. And as parents approach it prayerfully and sincerely, with the love of their whole hearts, it is a calling that carries with it a kind of intuition, inspiration, understanding, and insight—with a certain com-

[81]

mon sense and dedicated sincerity—for which there is no fully satisfactory substitute.

Of course children are trying and confining at times. But what better task can one be tied to than the nurturing and teaching and training of children, and helping to build good qualities of character? What more far-reaching task could one spend time on?

The apron strings should not be too tightly tied; nor yet left loose, to the point of irresponsibility or of wishing the children on others. Others can do much for which we may be grateful—agencies, institutions, individuals, schools, teachers, friends. But no one, individual or organization, can rightly take the place of competent, responsible parents. And no basic responsibility can supersede that of parents, nor is it something lightly to be set aside— for it was intended that parents and children should belong to each other, everlastingly. And being our children's keeper as well as our brother's keeper is one of the blessings and obligations and rewarding privileges that God has given.

A Mother, A Father—
Waiting

"The memory of a mother waiting is a safeguard against temptation." [73]

A mother, a father—a parent—who cares enough to wait and worry, who cares enough to counsel and to be concerned—is among the greatest blessings God has given. Of course young people may be impatient and wonder why parents want to know—need to know—where they go, what they do, the kind of company they keep: their activities, attitudes, and interests, and the course of life they intend to take. But in the complexity of our problems it becomes increasingly apparent that a loving, healthy, happy family is one of the most steadying factors in life and one of the surest sources of safety.

There are always temptations—always there are those who coax and dare and try to persuade young people to depart from safe principles and practices. There are evils and errors, heartaches and heartbreaks, wasted time and wasted lives. And in young people there is always a measure of independence, of wanting to strike out to see and decide for themselves, which is altogether understandable.

[83]

But you who are young: Don't misjudge the motives of parents, or their experience or responsibility, or their cause for concern. In the words of one earnest writer: "Children do not know how their parents love them, and they never will till the grave closes over those parents, or till they have children of their own." [80] It is part of the responsibility of parents to teach, to train, to help prevent the making of mistakes, and to help youth prepare for a useful, happy future without the bitterness or penalties that come from ignoring principles that have long been proved in the past. And it would be improper for parents not to know their children's plans and purposes.

There may be irritations and irksome restrictions at times, or so it may seem. But in looking back there will be great gratitude for those who helped in avoiding serious, time-wasting, heartbreaking mistakes.

"The memory of a mother [or a father] waiting is a safeguard against temptation."

Mothers—and Their Need
To Be Needed

There comes to mind a gentle mingling of many thoughts on mothers, and it would be difficult to consider this subject without an intermixing of tender emotion. As the words of William Goldsmith Brown remind us: "The sweetest sounds to mortals given / Are heard in Mother, Home, and Heaven." [81]

There are times—early times and others—when a devoted, understanding mother is needed more than anything else in the world, a need so urgent and obvious as to make difficult its utterance.

Then the years pass, and for mothers there may come a great gap between feeling much needed and being needed less and less or feeling needed not at all—as Jean Ingelow's words suggest:

> To bear, to nurse, to rear,
> To watch and then to lose,
> To see my bright ones disappear,
> Drawn up like morning dews. [82]

For mothers there is need to know that they are needed, long after the period of complete dependence of their children is past—long after the time of tender nurturing and nourishing—long after children have past the early years of youth, even to the later years of life.

There is need for mothers waiting, watching, often worrying; mothers giving, doing, sharing, caring, and constantly encouraging. Mothers need to know that they are loved, wanted, and appreciated, just as a performer needs approval and applause. As one writer said half a century ago: "A woman can stand anything but being forgotten, not being needed." [83]

Mothers bless and *are* blessed by having an essential part in the daily lives of loved ones. And so the years should endlessly remind us how much they do, or have done; how much they mean and have meant, how much they now must mean. There is need for all of us to know, as families, how much we need each other always. For the family is forever; this awareness comes when a loved one leaves, as Temple Bailey has sensitively suggested in these lines:

"Where's Mother?" could be heard through the hallway. And they stood and watched her as she went on alone, and the gates closed after her. And they said: "We cannot see her, but she is with us still. A mother like ours is more than a memory. She is a Living Presence." [84]

A Word to Fathers—and about Them

For this subject, we turn to the sincere and moving words of two sons who honored their fathers by honoring their own obligations and opportunities.

"Looking back," Roger W. Babson said of his father, ". . . I cannot help thinking how utterly wasteful of advice children are. . . . We usually are either too busy or too proud to ask for [it]. . . . Surely this is a great mistake. . . . But today it is too late. His spirit has fled. No wealth nor power can call it back. . . . Those of you . . . who have parents . . . talk things over with them more than you do. . . . Someone else can take your place in almost every other job excepting in the job of being a faithful son or daughter. One word to fathers: Don't wait too long before taking your children into your confidence. Don't figure that you'll know . . . [there] will be time enough. . . . This very night . . . open to them your heart. . . . Our families do not want us to leave them with a bigger business. They want more of us. . . . We have only a few years here at most. Let us use them sensibly and quit chasing one another like squirrels in a cage. . . . No other person in the whole wide world can take our place in the . . . home. . . ." [35]

Thomas Carlyle said of his father what each of us perhaps would wish to say: "Nothing that he undertook to do but he did it faithfully and like a true man. I shall look on the houses he built with a certain proud interest. They stand firm and sound. . . . I owe him much more than existence, I owe him a noble inspiring example. . . . His death was unexpected? Not so; every morning and every evening, for perhaps sixty years, he had prayed to the Great Father in words which I shall now no more hear him impressively pronounce, 'Prepare us for those solemn events, death, judgment, and eternity.' He would pray also, 'Forsake us not now when we are old and our heads grown gray.' God did not forsake him. . . . Let me not mourn for my father, let me do worthily of him. . . . Let me . . . walk as blamelessly through this . . . world, if God so will, to rejoin him at last. . . . God give me to live to my father's honor, and to His. And . . . in the world of realities may the Great Father again bring us together in perfect holiness and perfect love!" [56]

To Be a Son—To Love
a Father

A thoughtful young man said recently with grateful, heartfelt sincerity that he had "never spent sweeter or happier hours in life than in his father's home." Would that every son could say so, for this, in fact, is the pattern of life and its purpose: to learn well, work well, serve well, live well, with a balancing of life, and then to return to our Father's house, where once we were.

And now we recall some things said and some lessons learned from fathers lovingly remembered:

Of John Wallace Hamilton a grateful son said: "He was there if anything happened—not just physical mishaps, but those inner things not expressed. . . ." This must be one of the eternal attributes of a father: "He was there if anything happened." This is true of the Father of us all. He is there for us to find Him, to approach Him in prayer.

Hamilton said that his father held out strong, work-worn hands to the girl he was to marry: "These hands are clean hands," he said. "I offer them to you." [86] What a great and blessed thing for a father to offer as heritage for his children—clean, honest hands, with a willingness to work.

Carlyle said after his father had left this life: "Strange time—endless time; . . . All rushes on. Man follows. . . . I shall now no more behold my dear father with these bodily eyes. . . . His simple, true counsel and fatherly admonitions have now first attained their fit sacredness of meaning. Pity for me if they be thrown away. . . . His trust in me, was great. . . . He did nothing that was not kind and fatherly. . . . I have been a happy son. . . . Perhaps my father . . . is even now near me, with me. . . . Perhaps, if it so please God, we shall in some higher state of being meet one another, recognize one another. . . . Thank Heaven, I know and have known what it is to be a son; to love a father. . . . God give me to live to my father's honor and to His. . . ." [56]

Blessed is the son who could say, "I have spent no sweeter or happier hours than in the house of my father." And the father who can say, "I have given the world a clean, honest, God-fearing son." [87]

Oh, Why Do We Delay
So Much . . . ?

After the loss of a cherished loved one, Carlyle wrote in his reminiscences: "Alas! her love was never completely known to me . . . till I had lost her. Oh, for five minutes more . . . [with] her . . . to tell her with what . . . love and admiration, . . . I did . . . always regard her! . . . How good and tender she was, . . . Oh, why do we delay so much . . . ?" [56]

This puts us in mind of mothers—we who have lost them—and somehow seems to bring us a sense of things we didn't do. Oh, for five minutes more, to tell her of our love and our too often unexpressed awareness of all she was!

We remember cupboards that always held some sustenance when we came home hungry. We remember nights when we returned too late; but she was always awake and waiting. We remember picnics, and the tired homecoming when she—who had much more reason to be weary—would help us with knotted shoelaces or stubborn buttons and see us settled into sleep, and then attend to countless household chores before she thought of sleep herself.

We remember things she afforded us which she wouldn't afford for herself; the places she helped us to go, where she did not go, and her pleasure in hearing of our pleasure when we returned to tell what we had seen and done.

We remember cool, clean sheets, and the wearisome labor of washing them—and clean, fresh clothes, hung out sometimes in the heat of summer, sometimes in the cutting wind of winter, when the hands that hung them were blue and aching with cold.

We remember arms held open for us when we were hurt, hopes held high for us when we were down and discouraged, and quiet comfort for our disappointments, and sustaining strength and faith for our future.

We remember sorrows shared, and confidences that were always kept. We remember cool, quieting hands and comforting encouragement in fever and illness; tempting foods fixed for us, sleep lost for us, and prayers said for us. We remember prayers spoken at her knees, and her own prayers to an Eternal Father who did not fail her. All this and much more we remember of Mother.

And you who have mothers with you yet, will you not say with us as Carlyle said of his lost loved one—only say it sooner: "Thanks, darling, for your shining words and acts. God reward thee, dear one!"

"Oh, why do we delay so much?"

Speech—It Hurts or Heals

"Words as hard as cannon-balls . . ."
—Ralph Waldo Emerson [88]

Speech—It Hurts or Heals

In every successful relationship in life, three things are of particular importance: what we say, how we say it, and what we leave unsaid. And along with what we sometimes wish we *had* said there is also often what we wish we hadn't said. Most of us have reason to repent of having said what we shouldn't say—what, indeed, we perhaps never intended to say.

Many whose thoughts are significant have expressed themselves on the subject of silence and of too much talk:

"It is a great misfortune," Erasmus remarked, "not to have sense enough to speak well, and judgment enough to speak little." [89]

"If any man think it a *small* matter to bridle his tongue," said Plutarch, "he is much mistaken . . ." [90]

"Think *all* you speak," said Patrick Delany, "but speak not *all* you think. Thoughts are your own; your words are so no more." [91]

George Eliot once said: "Half the sorrows of women would be averted if they could repress the speech they know to be useless—nay, the speech they have resolved not to utter." [71] The same might well be said with equal truth of men.

Freedom of speech does not mean freedom from consequences. Speech is a form of action. It may hurt or heal. It is true or false, kind or cruel. It has its impact on others. And, said Samuel Johnson, "A man has no more right to say a rude thing to another than to act one; no more right to say a rude thing to another than to knock him down." [92]

We can all think of things we could cuttingly say—things that could put people in their place. But we can also think of things we have said that we have deeply regretted and would give much to take back. There are times when it is best to talk and times when it is blessed to be silent. We all have a responsibility to communicate, to get through, and to understand. And we are responsible for what we say, as well as for our silence.

Truth, Half-Truth, and Subtle Suggestion

Words are often overworked to exaggerate or overemphasize, and often also to deceive by half-truth or by subtle suggestion. A half-truth can in fact obscure the whole truth. A half-truth can effectively suggest a falsehood. The persistent repeating of half-truths can, for example, make things seem desirable or harmless which are in reality unwholesome and injurious, merely by a certain sophistry or suggestion.

"If any man seeks for greatness," said Horace Mann, "let him forget greatness and ask for truth, and he will find both." [93]

It is not glamor or surface considerations that make for greatness—or for truth—and not necessarily what is popular, or fashionable, or generally being done. These are often mere surfaces to cover a shallow substance. Words are often deliberately used to create an image merely for effect, merely for a front. Sometimes words are deliberately made to create misunderstanding—to distort and deceive and to create a false sense of security. There are some phrases from the Psalms suggestive of this subject: "The words of his mouth were smoother

[97]

than butter, but war was in his heart: his words were softer than oil, yet were they drawn swords." [94]

As with words and ideas, so with products or practices urged upon people: they must be honest products or practices—honest in purpose, beneficial in effect. They must be what they are said to be, must do what they are said to do. Guarantees or agreements must be words of truth and of actual intention. They must meet the final test of fact: whether or not what is said to be is or is not so.

Beyond words, beyond half-truths, beyond cleverness, concealment, and subtle suggestion we always need the final test of fact—what is intended, what is done, what is said or suggested, what actually *is or is not so*. Half-truths or deceptive suggestions are never safe substitutes for the whole truth —for honest, open facts.

"Is Not the Truth the Truth?"

Pilate's question to the Savior of mankind appears ever more important: "What is truth?" [95]
Much of the difficulty and disappointment of life comes because we either don't know the truth or don't live the truth we know. Much of our time is taken in searching for truth. Much of our trouble comes because we don't always know who is telling the truth. Much of our effort is spent in speculating, arguing—advocating theories, suppositions, hypotheses, and personal opinions or prejudices which we presume to be true. All this—or some of it—seems necessarily so because there is so much that is not now known.

But aside from what is known, and aside from the necessary searching for the unknown, there is always the question of deliberate deception—not innocent deception or the untruth of ignorance (bad as this may be), but deliberate deceit, in which the falsifier knows that he is falsifying about people, products, principles, for one motive or another—for power or profit or some other purpose.

Scripture has harsh things to say concerning the falsifier, which it would be well sometime to cite, in a day when so many seem dedicated to misleading the minds of men—when the war of words is being so fiercely fought. Nor have thoughtful persons outside of Scripture overlooked the subject.

"Truth," said Mark Twain, "is the most valuable thing we have." [96]

"Do not let us lie at all," wrote John Ruskin. "Do not think of one falsity as harmless, and another as slight, and another as unintended. Cast them all aside; they may be light and accidental, but . . . it is better that our hearts should be swept clean of them." [97]

"Nothing gives such a blow to friendship," wrote William Hazlitt, "as detecting another in an untruth. It strikes at the root of our confidence ever after." [98]

Falsehood causes sorrow, mistakes, waste, heartbreak, anguish, misguided lives. It is a thing of the Devil himself, who is the father of darkness and lies from the beginning.

Nor does truth seem to fare well in every encounter. Certainly it is not always seen or known, believed or accepted—so great is the power of deception. But let those who have been wronged, deceived, defrauded, injured, or misguided be strengthened by this assurance from Oliver Wendell Holmes: "Truth is tough. It will not break, like a bubble, at a touch." [99] Truth *is* tough. It will emerge and it will triumph.

Shakespeare seems almost to have been replying to Pilate's question, when he asks in turn, "Is not the truth the truth?" [100]

"Neither Lie One to Another"

Truth or untruth is not always a matter of language, but often one of implication, inflection, innuendo. A clever person intent on being untruthful can give a false impression, even with the right words. This could perhaps be called *inner* untruth, the untruth of intention. A perceptive woman once said that she had less respect for those who pride themselves on sticking to the truth since she had come to realize how many people use "truthful" words in such a way as to convey a lie.

Concerning eloquence and oratory Carlyle has commented along this line—and it applies in principle to any utterance, public or private: "What has been done by rushing after fine speech! . . . I want you to study Demosthenes, and to know all his excellences. At the same time, I must say that . . . he advised next to nothing that proved practicable; much of the reverse. Why tell me that a man is a fine speaker, if it is not the truth that he is speaking? . . . For, if a 'good speaker' . . . is not speaking the truth . . . but the untruth . . . is there a more horrid kind of object in creation? . . . Really it is not the speech, but the thing spoken that I am anxious about! I really care very little how the man said it provided I understand him and it be true." [101]

"Beware of Affectation in speech," wrote William Penn. "It often wrongs Matter, and ever shows a blind side." [102]

"Truth," said another source, "is the secret of eloquence and of virtue, the basis of moral authority; it is the highest summit of art and life." [103]

"It is sophistry," wrote Walter Lippmann, "to pretend that in a free country a man has some sort of inalienable or constitutional right to deceive his fellow men. . . . It may be inexpedient to arraign every public liar, as we try to arraign other swindlers. . . . But, in principle, there can be no immunity for lying in any of its . . . forms." [104]

Technical "truth" coupled with untruth of intention often seeks to deceive without seeming to deceive. But deceit is punishable in the court of conscience, where all things are accounted for, no matter how clever a man may be in his way with words.

We may fittingly recall the commandment from Leviticus: "Neither lie one to another." [105]

"Innocence" of Intent

Some two centuries ago, Jean Baptiste Massillon in *The Curse of a Malignant Tongue* posed some questions concerning innocence of intent: "What matters it to the brother whom you stab whether it be done through indiscretion or malice? Does an arrow, unwittingly drawn, make a less dangerous or slighter wound than if sent on purpose? . . . It is here he ought to put a guard of circumspection on his tongue, weigh every word, put them together in his heart, says the sage Ecclesiasticus, and let them ripen in his mouth. . . ." [106]

Those who have done damage often say they didn't mean to do it—loose talkers, for example, whose words do damage, or loose doers whose deeds do damage. And besides the talkers there are also the listeners, concerning whom August Hare asked, and answered his own question: "When will talkers refrain from evil-speaking? When listeners refrain from evil-hearing." [107]

"There would not be so many open mouths," said another observer, "if there were not so many open ears." [108]

There are times when any or all of us could be critical of others, or misjudge them, or say or do what we shouldn't. Then later we say we are sorry, sincerely so, and wish—oh, how we sometimes wish! —we could take back something said or something done.

To turn again to Massillon: "We would not wish to tarnish a man of character, . . . that would be too infamous and mean: . . . [yet] I know that it is, above all, by the innocency of the intention that they pretend to justify themselves; . . . But . . . where is the innocency of an amusement [when] . . . in effect, you excuse the malignity of your . . . tongue by the innocency of your intentions?" [106]

Of course we are sometimes sorry, and in some measure may not have intended to say what we said or to do what we did—but must we not remember that the hurt, the unmeant damage, cannot be completely recalled?

"Does an unintended arrow make a less dangerous wound than if sent on purpose? [We] ought to put a guard of circumspection on [the] tongue, [and] weigh every word."

"The Curse of a Malignant Tongue"

"What is the cruel pleasure which carries sorrow and bitterness to the heart of your brother? . . . Whence comes it that your sarcasms are always pointed to . . . recalling his faults . . . ? Where is the innocency of an amusement whose source springs from . . . [that] which ought to inspire you with compassion and grief?" [106]

In other words, what moves men to find pleasure in the weaknesses and faults and inadequacies of others? These searching questions come from some lines of Massillon on innocence of intention, and he continues: "May it not proceed from . . . jealousy? Would Saul have so often repeated with such pleasure that David was only the son of Jesse, had he not considered him as a rival? . . . Is it not your wish to render yourself agreeable, by turning your brother into an object of contempt and ridicule? 'Edify each other,' says St. Paul, 'by words of peace and charity . . .' " [106]

Whatever the motive, who is really responsible for spreading gossip or rumor or unkind comment? Who is responsible for wrong impressions, for false reports?

First, there are those who start them—frequently by saying that "they say so," without identifying the source. Second, there are those who pass them on; these must share the responsibility, since every link in any chain plays its part. To use a figure from another field: first someone makes the product; secondly, someone distributes it; and third, others receive or accept it. Production, distribution, consumption: in gossip, in rumor, in false report it is essentially that simple, as suggested by these lines from Alexander Pope:

> The flying rumors gather'd as they roll'd,
> Scarce any tale was sooner heard than told;
> And all who told it added something new
> And all who heard it made enlargements too.[109]

In some degree this comes under the category of bearing false witness. Thus before we relay rumor, gossip, or irresponsible reports we should consider not only the source but also the probable effect—remembering that we cannot recall them, and remembering also that we are responsible not only for facts but for the psychological effect of any part we play in making things seem other than they are.

Whatsoever we pass on, we ourselves are responsible for our part of the performance—and we cannot shift responsibility altogether by declaring our innocence of intention.

Advice and How To Give It

There is a point of approach in all personal relationships that opens up a long list of subjects, and that is the *how* of things as well as the *what*—*how* things are said and done. Consider, for example, the giving and taking of advice, which are among the most delicate and difficult relationships of life.

"Advice is not disliked because it is advice," said Leigh Hunt, "but because so few people know how to give it." [110]

None of us has lived so long that he has no need to learn. There is not one of us who could not profit by counsel of consultation; but how it is given, how it is done, how criticism is offered—the spirit, the manner, the attitude, the kindly or cutting quality—the *how* of things—is exceedingly important in all of life's relationships.

"I wish well-meaning, sensible men," said Benjamin Franklin, "would not lessen their power of doing good by a positive, assuming manner, that . . . tends to create opposition, and to defeat every one of those purposes for which speech was given to us. . . . For, if you would inform, a positive and dogmatical manner in advancing your sentiments may provoke contradiction and prevent a candid attention. . . ." [111]

"Harsh counsels have no effect," said Claude Helvetius, "They are like hammers which are always repulsed by the anvil." [112]

We all need to seek and consider counsel. Children need it; parents need it; everyone needs it —personally and professionally, in matters both private and public. No one knows it all. No one is sufficient unto himself. Seeking and considering counsel is a source of strength and safety, and there is no use letting pride or anger or irritation prevent us from accepting what is for our good.

To his remarks about advice, cited above, Franklin adds, "They that will not be counselled, cannot be helped. If you do not hear reason she will rap you on the knuckles." [111]

"Life is but one continual course of instruction," [113] but those who would teach and tell others would do well to avoid an irritating, alienating attitude, and should counsel and correct with love, patience, and persuasion.

"A sound head, an honest heart, and a humble spirit," said Sir Walter Scott, "are the three best guides through time and to eternity." [114] And surely he who would advise others should give evidence of having all three.

Advice Is Like Snow . . .

Among the greatest needs of mankind is that of communication—understanding, getting through to people—not just words, but meanings; not just phrases, but spirit; not just speech, but heart. So many misunderstand so many—especially motives: why people do what they do, why they say what they say, and what they mean by what they say. And failure in giving effective counsel is frequently failure in communicating the real meanings and motives.

Advice, in the first place, usually implies that something is wrong, that something is being criticized, that something should be changed. "One of life's greatest paradoxes," said Milton Sills, "is that nearly everyone wants to improve his circumstances but hardly anyone wants to improve himself." [115] Or, as Samuel Johnson said it: "Advice is seldom welcome. Those who need it most, like it least." [92]

Certainly no one likes it if it is given in the wrong way. And so often words get in our way, for the same words don't always mean the same thing to different people, not even sometimes in the same household: between husband and wife, between parents and children, or between the children. Nor, in fact, under different circumstances, do the same words always carry the same meaning even to ourselves. Furthermore, the pressures of life often prevent us from giving due attention to the subtleties and sensitivities of some situations, and we often blunder with words and walk roughshod where we should have approached with delicacy and deference.

Yet we need to talk, to communicate, to understand and to know that what friends and loved ones tell us is usually well intended. Children and young people need to know this and not resent counsel. By listening and heeding they could save themselves many heartaches, and one longs to plead with them to listen, to consider, to accept; for even when advice is not without irritation, it is the substance that counts, the truth, the intention.

We would also plead with parents to have understanding and patience in the *how* of what needs to be said.

As to all of this, Coleridge commented: "Advice is like snow; the softer it falls the longer it dwells upon, and the deeper it sinks into the mind." [116]

* * *

"When death, the great reconciler, has come, it is never our tenderness that we repent of, but our severity."

—George Eliot [71]

In Spending Time We Spend Ourselves

"The Future is something which everyone reaches at the rate of sixty minutes an hour, whatever he does, whoever he is."

—C. S. Lewis [117]

Eliminating the Insignificant

Time is *limited,* and the things that would take our time are *limitless.* We need to "eliminate the insignificant." [118] We need to be more selective in our choices, more discriminating as to trivia, more attentive to the things that mean most—for we never have time enough to do all we want to do or ought to do. As John Burroughs said, "I still find each day too short for all the thoughts I want to think, all the walks I want to take, all the books I want to read, and all the friends I want to see." [119]

Aside from all that presses in the present, we must also take time to pause and plan and think ahead for the future. When we shoot at a moving target, we must shoot ahead if we are to hit the mark. If we are only trying to meet the immediate moment, we see things only as they are—partly or altogether past. Many centuries ago Seneca said: "Even if we paid strict attention, life would soon get ahead of us; but as we are now, life finds us lingering and passes us by as if it belonged to another, and though it ends on the final day, it perishes *every* day." [120]

We have to take time to think, to reflect, to appraise the past, to explore beyond the present, to plan the future. "There must be," as Massillon said, "a

certain desire of improvement and of acquiring instruction; a serious turn of mind, opposed to everything frivolous; a habit of retirement and reflection;
a methodical arrangement of life: . . ." [121] And the
faster the pace and the greater the pressure, the
more we need solid foundations and our roots down
deep.

We have to live thoughtfully and be discriminating as to everything that takes our time. We must
eliminate the insignificant, the inconsequential,
the irrelevant. We must not let our lives be broken
into small pieces that get lost along the way, but
live so that we can see a pattern, a plan, a purpose
—so that each motion and moment has meaning.

Reaction Time

" Spend your time in nothing which you know must be repented of," said an English divine.[122]

Many if not most of our problems come with misuse of time—not only time in its continuing flow, but in the decisions or reactions of a single second. Studies of reaction time indicate how vitally important even part of a second can be. In the use of side arms, for example, the difference between those who live and those who die is frequently a fraction of a second. The same could no doubt be said for the days of swords and spears— and certainly it may be said for these days of highway hazards, where at 60 miles an hour a car travels 88 feet in a single second.

Thus the difference between life and death, good and evil, safety and sorrow—between a quiet or unquiet conscience—between what can or cannot be recalled—is often only an instant. This is true of utterance as well as action. A second's thought before we say something would leave many things blessedly unsaid. A second's thought before we do something would leave many unwise things undone. The ill-advised action or utterance can lead to incalculable consequences.

There is no problem in filling time. The demands, invitations, urges, interests, and opportunities of life pull us in a thousand different directions. It is a question of using time for what we should; for what is immediately necessary, and for what is of permanent, everlasting value. And we have to strike a balance between the two.

"Do not spend money for that which is of no worth, . . . nor your labor [or life or time] for that which cannot satisfy." [123] We need time to think, to explore, to reach for the real essentials; to pursue an honest search, ever seeking to come closer to the answers that evade us and to an understanding of eternal truth. The thoughtful use of time with honest intent gives peace and a deep and satisfying assurance to the soul.

Balance, Moderation, Judgment

"Whatever men attempt," said Bernard Baruch, "they seem driven to overdo." [124] It is true that there are extremes and excesses in all directions and endeavors. It reminds one of Dostoevsky's young man who knew that he had only a little time to live: "I couldn't endure the scurrying, bustling people," he said, "everlastingly dreary, worried and preoccupied, flitting to and fro about me on the pavement." [125] This flitting, scurrying busy-ness in matters both great and small is a familiar picture and impression as one pulls aside and pauses to consider the scene.

Any significant accomplishment requires conviction, concentration, dedication—a kind of all-out effort. But any truly successful life also requires balance. The gift of moderation, judgment—balance—is a great and important gift.

People have various ways of going to extremes. Some plunge and speculate inordinately, while others are too timid to venture at all. Some scatter their efforts and interests in too many directions; others move with such narrowness that they lose all breadth of life and neglect family, friends, and many of the things that matter most. Some overdo optimism to the point of not facing facts. Some overdo pessimism to the point of ignoring their best opportunities. Some live too much on the physical side, too absorbed in exercise and activity; others withdraw within themselves in inactivity. Some have too much desire for money, and some are too little concerned with solvency and the practical side.

The fact that God gave us minds and spirits, hearts and feelings, as well as physical functioning must mean that He meant us to be mindful of all sides of ourselves. The fact that He has given us both time and eternity must mean that we should give balance to both and to all that makes up man— "with prudence and thanksgiving" [126] in whatever we do or partake of, in every act and utterance.

We must specialize and concentrate to the point of being effective and efficient, but not to the point of starving any side of ourselves. We should avoid excesses and obsessions, or overdoing in any direction. "Whatever men attempt, they seem driven to overdo." We ought earnestly to come closer to balance, to solvency and soundness, to happiness and good health; and we ought to pause long enough to appraise what is of lasting importance to our lives.

To Have Health . . .

In facing a fatal illness, one of Dostoevsky's characters has some searching things to say about health: "Oh, now I don't care, now I've no time to be angry, but . . . how I used to dream . . . how I longed to be turned out into the street . . . to be deserted and utterly alone, without lodging, without work, without a crust of bread, without relations, without one friend in a great town, hungry, beaten . . . but healthy . . . then I would show them." [125] This poignant utterance on the matchless blessing of health suggests much that is sobering.

Ill health may come, of course, through unavoidable misfortune; but it can also come, unfortunately, from neglect, indifference, indulgence, uncontrolled appetites and harmful habits, and a variety of avoidable circumstances and situations—and this is the more pity, since this wondrously functioning physical frame, given us by God, is precious beyond price.

What fine, interacting function there is between spirit and mind and body, and all else that makes up a man! No one can fully define it or draw sharp lines of separation, but whatever is temporal, whatever eternal, there should be intelligent use, intelligent care toward healthy, happy, effective functioning, without cluttering mind or spirit or our physical faculties with what is known not to be good for man.

We have an obligation to know the laws of health so far as we can and to live temperately— with prudence and thanksgiving, with respect and gratitude, avoiding anything that would make us less than wholesomely alive or responsibly alert. It is utter unwisdom to do what would make us less than our healthiest and happiest.

Respect, caution, and common sense should keep us from indulging or abusing or ignoring the wondrous, finely functioning physical faculties that God has given us—the only ones we will ever have within the limits of this life.

"Read the Best Books First"

Of all the uses of time, some surely should be taken for reading—time for acquaintance with great thoughts, great minds, great men. But what we read is of incalculable consequence, for books vary in quality and character: some true, some false; some virtuous, some salacious; some uplifting, some degrading. Indeed, books are likely to be like the men who make them, and we would scarcely recommend exposing ourselves or our children to *every* man's mind. In choosing what to read, as in choosing what to eat, we should be discriminating lest the substance be unfit for food.

"You require judgment in the selectors of books," said Carlyle, "real insight into what is for the advantage of human souls, the exclusion of all kinds of clap-trap books which merely excite the astonishment of foolish people. . . ." [101] "We talk of food for the mind, as of food for the body," wrote John Ruskin, "now a good book contains such food inexhaustible . . . [but] no book is worth anything which is not worth much. . . ." [127] "Books are the best of things, well used," said Emerson. "Abused [they are] among the worst." [128] "We must be careful what we read," said John Lubbock, "and not, like the sailors of Ulysses, take bags of wind for sacks of treasures, . . ." [129]

"The very abundance of books in our days—a stupefying and terrifying abundance," wrote James Bryce, "has made it more important to know how to choose. . . . The first piece of advice I will venture to give you is this: Read only the best books. . . . Let not an hour . . . be wasted on third-rate or second-rate stuff if first-rate stuff can be had." [130]

It comes down essentially to this: that besides being a depository of the knowledge, discovery, and experience of the world, books are also a reflection of men's minds. They reflect the false as well as the true, the trivial as well as the profound, the degrading as well as the uplifting. Merely because something is put into print does not mean it is worth reading or can be believed. And as surely as men shall be held accountable for their acts and utterances, just so surely shall they be accountable for what they put into print.

Thus reading should always be selective and "out of the best books." [131] "Read the best books first," said Thoreau, "or you may not have a chance to read them at all." [132]

Books and the Company We Keep

Reading, while exceedingly important, is not an objective in itself. We should read for knowledge, for content and meaning, considering the substance and asking ourselves: Who wrote what, and why? Is it true or false? Is it wholesome or morbid? Is it poisonous, polluted? What is its impact, its impression, its message? In what direction does it move men?

"I have often been astonished," said John Lubbock, "how little care people devote to the selection of what they read. And yet many . . . read almost by hazard. They will take any book they chance to find in a room at a friend's house; they will buy a novel at a railway stall if it has an attractive title; indeed, I believe in some cases even the binding affects their choice." [129]

James Bryce recalls that "Goethe once said of someone, 'He is a dull man. If he were a book, I would not read him.'" And to this quotation from Goethe, Bryce added: "When you find that a book is poor, . . . waste no more time upon it." [130]

Ruskin writes of books as friends—and also as opportunities for appointments with people whose lives and thoughts are of surpassing importance. "We may, by good fortune," he said, "obtain a glimpse of a great poet and hear the sound of his voice; or put a question to a man of science . . . or snatch, once or twice in our lives, the privilege of throwing a bouquet in the path of a Princess, . . . meantime there is a society continually open to us, of people who will talk to us as long as we like . . . talk to us in the best words they can choose, and of the things nearest their hearts. And this society . . . can be kept waiting round us all day long—kings and statesmen [and prophets, he might have added] lingering patiently . . . in our bookcase shelves. . . . Books . . . have been written in all ages by the greatest men:—by great readers, great statesmen, and great thinkers. They are all at your choice; . . . Will you go and gossip with your housemaid, or your stable-boy . . . when all the while this eternal court is open to you . . . wide as the world, . . . [with] the chosen, and the mighty, of every place and time? Into that you may enter always; in that you may take fellowship." [127]

Surely there must be a better reason for reading anything than the mere fact that it appears in print. We should "seek . . . out of the best books . . . wisdom" [131]—not the false, the mediocre, the shallow, the sensational, but the best. "The worth of a book is to be measured by what you can carry away from it. . . ." [130] As Sydney Smith said: "Live always in the best company when you read." [133]

The Process of Bringing Things About

"Some men have thousands of reasons why they cannot do what they want to, when all they need is one reason why they can."
—Dr. Willis R. Whitney [134]

Bringing Things About

"Men give me some credit for genius," said Alexander Hamilton. "All the genius I have lies just in this: When I have a subject in hand, I study it profoundly. Day and night it is before me. I explore it in all its bearings. My mind becomes pervaded with it. Then the effort which I make the people are pleased to call the fruit of genius. It is the fruit of labor and thought." [135]

"There is no line of work—business or professional—" says a recent observer, "where anyone can hope to gain any degree of success without intensive work." [136] In a letter in 1875 Tchaikovsky wrote an impressive comment on the creative process: "Very often one must first overcome laziness and lack of inclination," he said. "Then there are various impediments. Sometimes victory comes easily, sometimes inspiration entirely escapes me. But I believe it is the duty of an artist never to submit, for laziness is a strong human trait, and nothing is more harmful to an artist than to let laziness get the better of him. One cannot afford to sit and wait for inspiration; she is a guest who does not visit the lazy but comes to those who call her." [137]

This is true not only of the artist, but also of the

artisan, the laborer, the student, the seeker after truth, the pursuer of every duty and every endeavor. The Lord does not ordinarily offer unearned or unsought handouts. "Seek, and ye shall find." [138] "Men should be anxiously engaged in a good cause, and do many things of their own free will. . . ." [139] The finding of truth, the improving of talents, the increase of competence, the enlarging of experience —adding to understanding—all that pertains to improvement must be sought, prayed for, worked for, and persisted in and pursued. Inspiration—competence, accomplishment, even conviction—"does not visit the lazy but comes to those who call her."

The "Sense of Process"

One of the essential factors in happiness is the habit—the privilege and principle—of willing work. Of this we may not be as fully aware as we once were. We like the good things, the necessities and something else besides. But with complex and mechanized processes, and with so much isolation from the source, we may sometimes not be clearly aware of the way by which so much is brought about.

In commenting on a somewhat unproductive person, one knowing observer said, "[She] has no sense of process. . . . She wants the result without doing any of the work that goes to make it." [140] This is a compelling subject—the "sense of process"—the awareness of the thought, the skills, the talents, the work; the organizing and managing effort and energy that goes into producing anything. With Providence as first provider, plus what all others do—some think, some plan, some invent, some save or risk capital, some add physical skill and effort—by all of this together, so much is brought into being.

Now here, from several sources, are some statements of awareness of the meaning of work:

"Labor is the divine law of our existence," said Mazzini.[141]

"Every man's task is his life-preserver," observed Emerson.[3]

"Work is as much a necessity to man as eating and sleeping," remarked the philosopher Humboldt.[142]

"Work is not a curse," said Calvin Coolidge, "it is the prerogative of intelligence, the only means to manhood, and the measure of civilization." [143]

"There is no truer and more abiding happiness than the knowledge that one is free to go on doing, day by day, the best work one can do. . . ." commented the English philosopher and historian, R. G. Collingwood.[144]

"None so little enjoy themselves, and are such burdens to themselves, as those who have nothing to do. —Only the active have the true relish of life," said John Jay, a signer of the Declaration of Independence and an early justice of the Supreme Court.[145]

"I have lived to know," said Adam Clarke, "that the great secret of human happiness is this: never suffer your energies to stagnate." [146]

"The greatest asset of any nation," added George B. Cortelyou, "is the spirit of its people, and the greatest danger that can menace any nation is the breakdown of that spirit—the will to win and the courage to work." [147]

In all we have, and in the much doing it takes to bring so much about, let us never lose the sense of process, nor fail to be a fairly contributing part of that process. "All growth depends upon activity." [143]

The Truth of What We Do

There is truth in writing, truth in speaking, the truth or untruth of what is put into print, and truth or untruth of intention.

There is also truth in working—truth in what we do. Honesty, truth, and integrity are inseparable. Though they are words of slightly different shading, each is a part of the whole complex of character, for a person cannot be said to be truthful if he is not honest also.

"Woe to that mind which wants [i.e., lacks] the love of truth!" wrote William Ellery Channing, ". . . truth is the light of Infinite Mind, and the image of God in his creatures. . . ." There is no greater defect than the lack of "reverential love of truth, a readiness to toil, to live and die for it. Let . . . man be imbued in a measure with this spirit; . . . let him learn to regard truth as more precious than his daily bread." [148]

These are noble and worthy words. But let us for a moment reduce them to tangible everyday terms: Is it truthful in any relationship to give less than fair value? Less work? Less pay? Less service? Less substance? Less consideration?

"Fidelity," said James Parton, "is seven-tenths of business success." [149]—and all of us are helpless in the absence of it, for the customer or patron cannot always know what time or material it takes to perform an essential service, or what the intrinsic value is of some substances. We all have to trust at times to the integrity of those who do for us what we cannot do for ourselves.

Is it truthful to put in parts that are not needed? To charge for what is not used? To do what need not be done? Needlessly to increase cost? To charge for what one does not do? To do less work, to give less service, than the compensation received—or to pay less than the work is worth?

These questions do not concern any particular class or occupation or trade or profession, or any particular segment of society. They concern every man in his dealings with every other.

There is no greater essential in business, in the professions, or in any occupation or relationship in life, than truth and integrity. And truth has to do with the wholeness of man—with his fairness, his honor, his honesty—in all his life, in all his work, and in all his ways. "Let man's life be true," wrote Robert Browning.[150]

To close with a line from Leviticus: "Ye shall not deal falsely." [105]

Heroes behind the Scenes

In thinking of heroic people one need not necessarily have in mind the heroes of history—not necessarily well-known people, past or present. One may think of those who quietly, consistently live their lives, carrying their problems, adjusting to their disappointments, meeting their obligations.

Think of mothers who do the daily round of duty, not unappreciated perhaps, yet often unthanked. Think of fathers who faithfully provide for their families. Think of those who meet discouraging debts—debts of necessity—often not their own, but of others. Think of those of modest or meager means who share what they have, who honor their obligations, and who give in gratitude to God.

Think of those who take time to teach and train children, their own and others; of those who nurse the sick, who comfort the sorrowing; of those in whose homes are the handicapped.

Think of those who care for their own and yet take others into their hearts and homes.

Think of those who have lost loved ones by death; and of those deserted and left alone to carry the burden of others, doing double duty, or much more. Think of those who have suffered delays and disappointments in their plans and purposes, but who go on from where they are, keeping faith in the future.

Think of those in every organization, in every effort, who do innumerable unnamed tasks, who assist behind the scenes and help to keep things going, the world over. For every leading part there is a supporting cast and many who are unseen, besides.

Think of those who humbly, prayerfully, approach their problems, who love truth, who resist cynicism; those who have turned from temptation; those who have made mistakes but have had the courage to repent, to turn back, to make amends.

There is great heroism in meeting life, in meeting problems, in serving, in sharing, in repenting, in keeping the commandments, in facing facts, in moving forward and not running away.

"Not a day passes over the earth," wrote Charles Reade, "but men and women of no note do great deeds, speak great words, and suffer noble sorrows. Of these obscure heroes, . . . the greater part will never be known till that hour when many that were great shall be small, and the small great." [152]

Great courage is required in the doing of each day's duty—and the Lord God will not forget those who do it—nor will He leave them alone.

To Begin—and Get Going

Few people, whether their life be long or short, start and go in a predetermined direction, without any detours or delays. But young people are sometimes discouraged by the difficulty of making decisions, by the difficulty of knowing what they want to be, what they want to do; and by interruptions and uncertainties, and the fear of failure. Yet this ought not to be so.

On this subject we quote some significant sentences written more than sixty years since—just in case the present generation should feel that such problems are peculiar to our particular time. "Few begin," says this source, "with anything like a clear view of what they want to do, and the fortune they seek may come in a very different form from that which they have kept in view." Those who are genuinely successful, the writer continues, "are those who are not paralyzed by failures. . . . While those who put all at risk on one venture, and, losing, weakly surrender, never accomplish anything worth living for. Failures [we might add, problems or interruptions] enter into the natural expectations of everybody. . . ." Everything depends on how we take our failures." [153]

We ought always to be earnestly "engaged in a

good cause," [139] to have a good purpose and pursue it. "Nothing is more unworthy of a wise man," said Plato, "or ought to trouble him more, than to have allowed more time for trifling and useless things than they deserved." [154]

The plain fact, restated for us all and especially for those younger in years, is that it is not given to any of us to see the end from the beginning, but we have to begin, we have to decide, we have to choose a good goal, and *we have to get going*. We have to accept the unavoidable interruptions, detours, delays; we have to be prayerful in decision, and patient and persistent in preparation.

"Few begin with anything like a clear view of what they want to do." But we have to choose a good objective and have the faith to prepare, to follow through—to be faithful in the small things of which the larger ones are mostly made.

A Question of Convenience

We turn to what could be called a question of convenience: the doing of things when they should be done, or dodging the doing of them —the whole habit of postponing, delaying, of learning only reluctantly, of withholding service, withholding self, withholding willing work.

The subject revolves essentially around this point: few things that require concentration, service, or extra effort ever seem to be quite comfortable or convenient. And a person who does not want to put himself out for anyone or anything can usually find an excuse for withholding himself or for feeling imposed upon.

No sincere self-improvement, no service to others, no calls that we respond to—personally or professionally—are ever quite convenient, if we don't consider them so. There are always other things we could be doing with our time, and if we are too self-satisfied or self-centered, or too little disposed to learn, work, study, serve; to accommodate, to extend ourselves, or to put out extra effort; we may acquire a chronic "don't-bother-me" attitude, always somehow supposing that it is easier for someone else to do what needs to be done.

But we all need others. We are all indebted to

others. All of us are served by others and should serve others. Moreover, we cannot develop by *not* doing. We cannot close ourselves up tightly and still be open for opportunity. We cannot learn without active effort. We cannot develop our full capacity without output on our part, without participation. If habitually we shrink from effort and obligation and opportunity, we shall surely stagnate and shrivel within our souls.

"Cast thy bread upon the waters: for thou shalt find it after many days." [155] If we are too afraid we may not get back what we give, we may never give enough to get. "He who saves his life shall lose it." [156] The truth is, we cannot save life—we can only use it. We can only stretch time by stretching ourselves. The parable of the talents is still in effect: what we do not use we can't increase.

This should commend to all of us an attitude of getting up and going—of entering in and doing—of settling down and learning—of getting in and serving—of getting out and working; of improving our knowledge, our work, our willingness, our capacity and productivity, our output and performance—and so stretching life by stretching ourselves, and not stagnating through an overemphasis on comfort or convenience.

* * *

"Out of the strain of the doing.
Into the peace of the done."
—Julia L. M. Woodruff [157]

Freedom . . . Force . . . and Silent Consent

"... What stands if freedom fall?"
—Rudyard Kipling [158]

Freedom . . . Cherished and Challenged

Since freedom is one of the most cherished and challenged rights in all the world, it is a subject most seriously to be considered. And while these words may have an all-too-familiar sound, it is not too soon to say again that freedom cannot always continue in comfort and convenience, cannot be assured without sacrifice, without truth and decency, without willingness to work, without downright honesty and honor, and readiness to keep the commandments and live within the law.

We may have our choice, but we cannot have both: we cannot have *both* liberty and indifference, or *both* liberty and licentiousness. There is no liberty without a real respect for law; no liberty if we forget God, or fail to remember the principles on which freedom is founded.

"To suppose that our civil and political liberties are secure because they are . . . defined in written constitutions," said Carl Lotus Becker, "is to mistake the legal form for the living substance of freedom." [159]

The institutions of our nation, observed John Foster Dulles, "reflect the belief of our founders

[141]

that men had their origin and Destiny in God . . . and had duties prescribed by moral law." [160]

"Bad men cannot make good citizens. . . ." said Patrick Henry. "It is when a people forget God, that tyrants forge their chains. . . . No free government. . . . can be preserved to any people but by a firm adherence to justice, moderation, temperance, frugality, and virtue." [161]

" . . . to obey God is perfect liberty," said Seneca. "He that does this shall be free, safe, and quiet. . . ." [162] Those are wonderful words: free, safe, and quiet.

"Liberty," said Woodrow Wilson, "has never come from government. . . . The history of liberty is a history of limitations of governmental power, not the increase of it." [163]

"Their venerable forms rise before us," said Charles Sumner of the generations that have gone. "They seem to speak to us, their children: 'Cease to vaunt yourselves of what you do. . . . Learn to walk humbly, and to think meekly of yourselves. Cultivate habits of self-sacrifice and of devotion to duty . . . never aim at aught which is not right . . . [else] every possession and all knowledge will become an evil and a shame. . . . To each generation is committed its peculiar task . . . let us turn our thoughts [to] the *character* of our country . . . and [practice] that righteousness which exalteth a nation. . . .' " [164]

Free, Safe, and Quiet

Freedom is basically something God-given, of which for certain purposes we delegate a part. History has proved it wise and prudent to limit what we in any degree delegate, and never to seek thereby to relieve ourselves of real responsibility. "There is no liberty," said Henry Ward Beecher, "to men who know not how to govern themselves." [151]

"I believe," said James Madison, "there are more instances of the abridgment of the freedom of the people by gradual and silent encroachment . . . than by violent and sudden usurpations." [165] "The true danger," Edmund Burke believed, "is, when liberty is nibbled away for expedients, and by parts." [166]

Seldom, if ever, does anything of consequence happen suddenly. There is a background and a beginning, and a progressive process: a little giving, a little compromising, a little trading for time—sometimes a little concession to comfort and convenience —a little sacrificing of principle for some supposed personal privilege or preference.

"Thank God, for the iron in the blood of our fathers," said Theodore Roosevelt. "No country can long endure if its foundations are not laid deep in the material prosperity which comes from thrift, from business energy and enterprise, from hard, unsparing effort in the fields of industrial activity, but neither was any nation ever yet truly great if it relied upon material prosperity alone. . . . Our debt is yet greater to [those who] . . . showed by their lives that they recognized the law of work . . . to win a competence for themselves and those dependent upon them." [167]

Free agency is among the most precious of man's possessions, among the most precious of God's gifts. Its preservation demands honor, reverence, and respect—and the acceptance of real responsibility. We recall again Seneca's voice speaking down the centuries: ". . . to obey God is perfect liberty; he that does this, shall be free, safe, and quiet." [162]

Freedom . . . Force and Silent Consent

Men rise heroically to violent threats, to rude attacks, to the sudden show of force, but often seem asleep to slow and subtle slipping.

Preoccupation with comfort and convenience, with personal privilege and problems, can lead—and often does—to a degree of complacency with which freedom is never assured or safe. Kahlil Gibran has given us some searching lines on this subject.

"In their fear your forefathers gathered you too near together. . . ." he wrote. "And tell me . . . what have you in these houses? And what is it you guard with fastened doors? Have you peace, the quiet urge that reveals your power? Have you remembrances, the glimmering arches that span the summits of the mind? Have you beauty, that leads the heart from things fashioned of wood and stone to the holy mountain? . . . Or have you only comfort . . . that stealthy thing that enters the house a guest, and then becomes a host, and then a master? . . . Though its hands are silken, its heart is of iron. It lulls you to sleep. . . . It makes mock of your sound senses, and lays them in thistledown like fragile vessels. Verily the lust for comfort murders the passion of the soul, and then walks grinning in the funeral." [168]

"There are two ways in which a people can lose their rights [that is, freedom]," wrote Robert Dunning Dripps. "One is by violence. . . . The other is by surrender or non-use, and there lies the great danger. . . . Every right has its . . . duty. Do you and I realize the extent to which we have been turning over . . . responsibilities and duties which it is ours and ours alone to perform? . . . Let us take out this . . . charter of our liberties . . . and perform our part of the agreement, in order that with clean hands we may stand upon the terms and provisions in which we have reserved and safeguarded our rights. . . ." [169]—as another writer puts it, "in the firm belief that God in his providence established this nation for a purpose . . . for the protection of the rights of man. . . ." [170]

What our fathers fought and died for, grant that we may be willing to live for, reaffirming our faith in the Constitution—"a glorious standard . . . a heavenly banner . . . founded in the wisdom of God" [171]—"by the hands of wise men whom [He] raised up unto this very purpose" [172]—the symbol and safeguard of our heritage of freedom, which, please God, we may never lose, either by force or by silent consent.

The Constitution of Our Country

Each hour we live we have more reason to be grateful for both liberty and law, and for the inspired Constitution that makes these priceless things possible. Except for an occasional look back into history or an occasional present comparison, we seem to have too little awareness of what the Constitution means in its safeguards to freedom and personal privacy.

Always there are those who would encroach upon men's liberties and lives; those who, if permitted, would intrude too much upon the freedom and privacy of people. "If men were angels," said James Madison, "no government would be necessary. . . . In framing a government which is to be administered by men over men, the great difficulty lies in this: you must first enable the government to control the governed; and in the next place oblige it to control itself." [173]

This is a delicate balance. There is no faultless wisdom among men, and no certainty as to the temperance of power or opinion. All are human; all make mistakes, and thus we need the safeguards, the checks and balances, that permit a maximum of

[147]

liberty within the essential minimum of law. And so we thank God for the free agency of man and for what, under Divine Providence, our fathers fashioned for us.

But—"Liberty lies in the hearts of men and women," said Judge Learned Hand. "When it dies there, no constitution, no law, no court can save it." [174]

Concerning the Constitution George Washington said: "It will be so much beyond anything we had a right to imagine or expect . . . that it will demonstrate as visibly the finger of Providence, as any possible event in the course of human affairs can ever designate it." [175]

"Let us take heed to our ways," said William Maxwell Evarts in 1876, "and while it is called today resolve that the great heritage we have received shall be handed down through the long line of the advancing generations." [176]

"Nothing is more shameful for a man," said Charles Sumner, "than to . . . enjoy it without transmitting it to the next generation." [164]

God grant that we may more often remind ourselves what our fathers fought for, lived for, died for: that "this land shall be a land of liberty." [177]— and, in Franklin's words, that "not only the love of liberty, but a thorough knowledge of the rights of man, may pervade all the nations of the earth. . . ." [178]

The Constitution—Old as Truth and Modern as Tomorrow

"If men were angels," we noted from James Madison, "no government would be necessary." And in framing a government of the people by the people, the great difficulty is that one must "first enable the government to control the governed; and in the next place oblige it to control itself." [173]

Since no man is infallible, since there is no guarantee of moderation in the use of power or opinion, the need for checks and balances seems self-evident —and the need for humility and understanding also. "Having lived long," said Benjamin Franklin, "I have experienced many instances of being obliged by better information or fuller consideration, to change opinions even on important subjects, which I once thought right, but found to be otherwise." [179]

All men may at times be mistaken—and in all our relationships with one another we need both the flexibility to give and take in personal opinion, and the firmness to preserve and safeguard sound principles.

[149]

The framers of the Constitution, said Ira Jewell Williams, "wanted . . . the maximum freedom of the individual consistent with respect for the rights of all. . . . Our . . . fathers did not want to be placed under legislative tutelage. They felt amply and splendidly able to take care of themselves. . . . Every new 'Thou Shalt Not,' . . . not only impairs individual initiative," added the writer, but its enforcement requires also enormous hordes of enforcers.[180]

So much for some opinions of the past. Now as to the present: The price of enjoying such privileges is that of accepting the responsibilities—both personal and public. We are all entitled to work out our own salvation in the blessed air of freedom, with understanding, temperance, and willingness to work; with liberty and respect for law, and with an awareness that "freedom and responsibility are inseparable." [181]

And here we reaffirm our faith that the Constitution our fathers fashioned for us is a divinely inspired document—founded on principles as old as truth, and yet as fresh and modern as tomorrow morning.

Thus Spoke Lincoln

There is much said concerning Lincoln—yet not too much for so great a subject. He is one of the great, even on the list of now immortal men.

As to some of his qualities of character, these were among the many: love, courage, integrity, humility—and there is no real greatness without any of these.

When he visited fallen Richmond, but a few days before he died, some whose cause he had served bowed down to him, while others fell at his feet. "This is not right," he said. "You must kneel to God only, and thank him for the liberty you will hereafter enjoy. I am but God's humble instrument." [182]

In one of the debates with Judge Douglas he said: "Our defense is in the spirit which prizes liberty as the heritage of all men in all lands everywhere. Destroy this spirit and you will have planted the seeds of despotism at our own doors. . . . Whether it is right or wrong to trample on the rights of others—that is the real issue . . . the eternal struggle between the two principles of right and wrong throughout the world." [183]

This he said in an appraisal of the dignity of people: "It is difficult to make a man miserable while he feels he is worthy of himself and claims kindred to the great God who made him." [184]

And this he said to the nation for which he gave his life: "Beware of rashness, but with energy and sleepless vigilance go forward . . ." [185] ". . . devoutly recognizing . . . Almighty God in all the affairs of men and nations. . . . It is the duty of nations as well as of men to own their dependence upon the overruling power of God, to confess their sins and transgression in humble sorrow . . . and to recognize the sublime truth . . . that 'those nations only are blessed whose God is the Lord.' . . . It behooves us then, to humble ourselves . . . and to pray for clemency and forgiveness. . . . All this being done in sincerity and truth . . . that the united cry of the nation will be heard on high." [186]

Thus spoke Abraham Lincoln, who lived and died with this prayer and purpose: "that this nation under God shall have a new birth of freedom . . . . and . . . shall not perish from the earth." [187]

God bless his memory, and ever preserve in righteousness the nation for which he was made a martyr.

Freedom Isn't Free

The question of the free agency of the individual is foremost among the issues confronting mankind at this moment—the principle around which revolve the absolute essentials of peace and progress, and of man's opportunity on earth—and, indeed, ever after. "The history of Liberty," wrote Edward Everett, "—the history of men struggling to be free . . . forms a subject which we cannot contemplate too closely. This is the real history of man." [188]

Also involved is the basic question of character—for coercion is not compatible with responsible, resourceful qualities of character. "The history of our time," wrote David E. Lilienthal, "will be written by what happens in the everyday lives of the men and women we see upon the streets and in the factories and on the farms and in the colleges and city halls and the legislatures and the administrative offices and the business establishments." [189]

In all the tension of these times let not the main theme be obscured, nor men's minds diverted to side considerations. We must ever remember what the issue is: free agency—liberty within law—the freedom to live as God gave men the right to live, responsible, resourceful, clean, honest; with truth and decency; with soundness and solvency, and with the moral and mental character to live in liberty within the law.

"No free government," wrote Andrew Jackson, "can stand without virtue in the people and a lofty spirit of patriotism." [190] And, said Somerset Maugham, "If a nation values anything more than freedom it will lose its freedom; and the irony of it is that if it is comfort or money that it values more, it will lose that too." [191]

The fact is—and we must face it—that freedom isn't free, isn't always comfortable, isn't always convenient; yet it is among the greatest of the gifts that God has given, for which we must be willing to work and to serve, not misled by lesser and incidental considerations, but with our eyes and efforts always on the basic issue: that "this land shall be a land of liberty" [177] and of law.

To cite a sentence from an eminent source: "Only the disciplined are free." [192]

* * *

"Long may our land be bright
With freedom's holy light:
Protect us by the might,
Great God, our King!"
—Samuel Francis Smith [193]

Thanksgiving, Christmas, and the Year's End

"Let every man search his heart and his life and consider . . . how good and gracious God has been."

—Editorial, *The Outlook* [33]

A Thoughtful, Thankful Season

Our thoughts turn again to a season of "maturity, ripeness, richness" [194] with an awareness of what the earth has accomplished, not only in providing plenty, but in giving added evidence of the goodness of Him who orders all things, and of the reasons we have to be humble. Indeed, it is doubtful whether there can be real gratitude without humility.

Life, the greatest of gifts, is sustained through the seasons by the growing of seed, the coming forth of the flower, and the fruit that follows. For this we are grateful. And since no man can make a seed or control the seasons, humility would seem to be a becoming quality.

What if even one harvest did not arrive on earth? What if the seasons did not follow in sequence? Let us thank God that He has brought us through another cycle of seasons, with seed to plant, and with the harvest we have.

"Gratitude," said Aesop, "is the sign of noble souls." [195] It is good to be grateful. But sometimes we are discouraged. Sometimes we are aware of adverse events. Sometimes we find fault. Yet since

[157]

"God would make us like himself, life is [an] exacting education. . . . [and beyond] gratitude for pleasant paths and fertile fields and surcease [from] anxiety, there ought to be [gratitude for the] gift of spiritual life which transforms . . . adversities into blessings, burdens into sources of strength . . . partings into prophesies of [happy] reunions." [33]

How can there be doubt, arrogance, insensitivity, or cynicism when we have the providence of God, the beauty of the earth, and awareness of our own smallness and of the greatness of our opportunities —with infinite truth to search for, and with the great assurances that God has given again at this time of "maturity, ripeness, richness"—a season that seems to say, "The fullness of the earth is yours!"

"No human counsel hath devised, nor hath any mortal hand worked out these great things," said Abraham Lincoln. "They are the gracious gifts of the Most High God, who, while dealing with us in anger for our sins, hath nevertheless remembered mercy. . . . [for which we] should be solemnly, reverently" grateful—"for singular deliverances and blessings . . . with humble penitence." [196]

Thanks—for All This

Surely it is gracious and proper to thank people whenever they perform a service. This we should take care to remember, in every household and every relationship in life, and in thanking others always. Service would be dull drudgery if there were no appreciation or thanks for it.

And since receiving thanks is so important to people, how much more important are our frequent thanks to the Father of us all, the Provider of all, who gave us life and loved ones, who keeps the seasons constantly recurring and keeps creation in its course.

"In every honest man there is an instinctive feeling that there ought to be some relation between the gift and the worth of the recipient. . . . He who receives a gift worthily always asks himself what he has done to deserve [it] . . . Perhaps the finest part of a gift is the searching of soul which it brings with it; and the greater the gift, the more frankly ought the man who receives it to [search] himself." [197]

This being so, we would here do some inner searching, and besides our obligation to all others, past and present, and especially to loved ones with whom we live, we would offer gratitude to God

[159]

for the rising of the morning sun, for the hopeful dawning of each day, for the beauty of the earth, for fertile fields; for health, for life, for law, for the love of loved ones; for truth, intelligence— "for the open doors of schools and universities" [198]— for the God-given right of freedom of thought, of action, of utterance, and for the patriots who have helped to preserve it; for work to do; for the kindly softening that follows the acuteness of a sorrow; for repentance and forgiveness, for the privilege of improving.

And may we give thanks not only "for finished harvests . . . for completed achievements . . . for work done," but for work yet to do, and "for men to lift themselves into the light . . . for the things which make for the healing of the world; not only for the life that has been lived, but for the boundless life that is to be . . . for the great open door of the future. . . ." [198]—for the great plan and purpose, for the promise of limitless possibilities and of life and loved ones everlastingly.

"Let every man search his heart and his life and 'consider . . . how good and gracious God has been.'" [33]

"Let the Nation Search
Itself . . ."

The theme of gratitude need not—should not—be confined to one day, one week. Thanks are always in season, beyond any season that may be set aside. And so we turn to a wider searching of ourselves, not only personally but as a people, and cite some meaningful sentences which, some sixty years ago, appeared in print, yet seem to have a message for this moment:

"It is a time, not for exaltation, but for searching of the conscience, for humility of spirit, for the heartfelt prayer of the whole people for light, for guidance, for strength, for sanity, for that passion for righteousness which consumes all pride, scorn, arrogance, and trust in the things that perish." [197]

"Some of us have grown so critical in spirit . . . that we forget how precious they [our inestimable blessings] are and how recently they have been bestowed. . . . It is given only to the spiritually-minded to understand a country like ours, as it is given only to the spiritually-minded to transform it from prophecy into achievement." [198]

"Therefore, let the Nation search itself as never before to discover if it be worthy of these great gifts." [197] And thus let us plead and pray: "Almighty God, who in former time leddest our fathers forth . . . give Thy grace . . . to us their children, that we may always . . . do Thy will. Bless our land with honorable industry, sound learning, and pure manners. Defend our liberties; preserve our unity. Save us from violence, discord, and confusion . . . and from every evil way. . . . Endue with the spirit of wisdom those whom we intrust in Thy name with the authority of goverance, to the end that there may be peace at home and that we keep our place among the nations of the earth. . . . Temper our self-confidence with thankfulness" [197]—and our fear with courage and faith. Then let us on our knees thank God for all that He has given.

Manna . . . and Men . . .

In speaking of gratitude and the giving and getting of gifts, we cite some thoughts from a source of half a century or so ago:

"If the end of society is to produce the largest number of free human spirits, of generous human hearts, of strong human hands, of pure human homes, of noble human lives . . . the setting free of those who are in bondage . . . care and reverence for . . . man as a man, the open door to the boy and girl whose feet are eager to climb . . . then let us reverently thank God that we were born in an age and [time] in which it is our supreme good not to be 'ministered unto but to minister' " [198]—not only to get, but to give.

As we think of all the needs of all people—of those who have been denied the great gift of freedom, or even food enough, or the privilege of learning; denied even the simplest literacy, so-called—when we think of the problems, the sorrows, and the needs, we may know how good it is to have been blessed with the opportunity for giving service, giving substance, and giving ourselves. And when we pray for others, may God help us in part to answer our prayers through our own earnest efforts—for He works many miracles and blessings by means of men.

Manna from heaven may come under some circumstances, but help from the hands of other men blesses both giver and receiver and is not necessarily costly: for it may be so simple, yet so great a gift, as counsel or companionship, or comfort, or the giving of talent or a little time, or simply showing an honest interest in others that makes them feel they are not alone in life. These sometimes are among the greatest gifts.

"Then shall the King say unto them . . . Come, ye blessed of my Father . . . For I was an hungered, and ye gave me meat: I was thirsty, and ye gave me drink . . . Naked, and ye clothed me: I was sick, and ye visited me: I was in prison, and ye came unto me. Then shall the righteous answer him, saying, Lord, when saw we thee an hungered, and fed thee? or thirsty, and gave thee drink? . . . or naked, and clothed thee? Or when saw we thee sick, or in prison, and came unto thee? And the King shall answer and say unto them, Verily I say unto you, Inasmuch as ye have done it unto one of the least of these . . . ye have done it unto me." [199]

The Words of Christmas

We have heard the sounds of Christmas, and have seen the sights of Christmas, and have felt the feelings of Christmas, and now for a moment may we mention the words of Christmas— words with which it is inseparably associated, such words as family, friends, fellowship and feasting; trees and trimmings; secrets and surprises; gifts and giving. At Christmas there are warmer feelings from stranger to stranger and from friend to friend, with always a mellowing influence, and with curt comment less likely to occur.

As a poet has put it: "Oh, somehow it seems to me that at Christmas, man is almost what God sent him here to be." [200]

There are other words that come to mind at Christmas: music and memories; beloved faces; vacant chairs; loved ones with us, loved ones away; home, and love, and peace—which are surely among the world's most wonderful words.

Scripture counsels us to "love one another," [201] to "love our neighbour," [202] to "love . . . the stranger," [203] even to "love our enemies," [204] to "love the Lord with all our hearts" [205]—and even to love ourselves, by living so as to have happiness.

And as to peace—peace within as well as without,

the peace of which the angels sang as they heralded the birth of the Prince of Peace—in such a time as ours we may well search ourselves to see what words are associated with peace. Peace is not passive but positive. It is service; it is sharing; it is fairness, honesty, cleanliness of thought and conduct; it is a clear and quiet conscience; it is freedom from quarreling and conflict; it is living within law, and it comes with loving men and proving it, and loving God and keeping His commandments.

And now the final word concerning Christmas: and that is Christ, without whom there would be no Christmas. Here and now we earnestly acknowledge from the deep certainty of our souls that Jesus is the Christ, the divine Son of God, the only begotten of the Father in the flesh, our Lord, our Savior, and Redeemer, who lived and died and came forth from death to life in a literal reality of resurrection. And with Job we would witness in these words: "I know that my Redeemer liveth." [206]

God bless us every one, and help us all to keep within our hearts and homes the words and spirit of Christmas, and to receive this day—and always—the great gift of personal peace.

Between Regret and Gratitude

Christmas has come and gone again, and its closeness leads us to the question: Could we not somehow keep the spirit that made Christmas so different a day? For different it was, as we well know. Could we somehow avoid repeating the cycle the poet has suggested?

> We ring the bells and we raise the strain,
> We hang up garlands everywhere,
> And bid the tapers twinkle fair,
> And feast and frolic—and then we go
> Back to the same old lives again.[207]

And now as we close another year, another succession of seasons, this is a time of looking two ways at once—a time almost of feeling two ways at once, as we move between regret and gratitude: regret for what we should have done and didn't, regret that so much more of life has come and gone, but gratitude that we have lived through yet another year, gratitude for the continuing of our lives, and that there is yet time for some of what we should be doing; gratitude for much that has not happened, that many of our fears have not taken tangible form; gratitude for the future.

Perhaps regret would be the dominating impulse

for us all if we would let it, because no one of us during the year past has turned in a perfect performance—of that we can be certainly sure. But whatever we have done or left undone, we must not live our lives in looking backward. Not forgetting lessons learned, we must turn around and face the future, using what truth, what facts we have, and living by faith where fuller facts are not as yet in evidence.

The fact is, we have come through another year with faith—have come through it, if not in perfect peace, at least in comparative peace. And still we have the sweet assurance, to use Robert Millikan's words, that "the Creator is still on the job." [208]

And so we end the old and face the new with faith. And as we face "the never-ending flight of future days," [209] our gratitude may overshadow our regret, if we present honest repentance for the past and a trusting, working faith for the future, while time moves on into the endless reaches of eternity— for God, who made us in His image, is mindful of us all and will lead us, with our willingness, to peace and progress, as He moves His eternal purposes "in His majesty and power." [210]

* * *

"Live for something.—Do good . . . Write your name in kindness, love, and mercy . . . year by year . . ."

—Thomas Chalmers [211]

Repentance, Improvement, and "Promise-Making to the Future"

> "One must separate from anything that forces one to repeat No again and again."
>
> —Nietzsche [212]

Our Sincere Resolves

"There are times when we have a more or less conscious feeling of turning over a new leaf, of getting a fresh start, . . . and this consciousness is usually accompanied by a more or less definite determination [to do better, to be better] . . . Later . . . there may be a time when we repent of our repentance." [213]

These words, written half a century ago, remind us "of many failures to carry out contracts that people have made with themselves. . . . This is the time of danger, when the strength of our resolution is put to the test. If we give way . . . we lose ground; . . . To lose confidence in other people is disheartening, to lose the confidence of other people is painful, but to lose confidence in one's self is fatal." [213] This often comes from attempting too much, from resolving too rashly. Sudden declarations, extreme statements, impetuous proposals, the sudden solemn swearing that we will do this or that if it's the last thing we do, are frequently the prelude to departure from the proposed practice or improvement. It is often better to do calmly and quietly what we can, rather than to vow that we will do more than is reasonably possible. "It is [as] important to keep the promises you make to yourself [as] those you make publicly." [213]

Yet even when resolutions are unwisely made, without inward readiness, or without a full knowledge of the facts, they should not suddenly be abandoned simply on impulse, but "abrogated (if at all) only after serious deliberation of our higher selves." They should not be "cast aside in a moment under stress of the very temptation against which they were intended to guard." [213] It is well to resolve well, but it is not a good thing to resolve rashly and then rashly retreat from resolve.

Consistency and continuity are the real shapers of character, the real producers of improvement. Quiet, prayerful determination to do better and be better is more fruitful than boastful declarations of what we are about to be or about to do.

God grant us the quiet constancy of character to resolve what we should, and then to see it through.

Breaking the Chain of Temptation

"The best of us resolve to do better, and the worst of us resolve it even more stringently," said one understanding observer. "That is the curious and pathetic thing about this promise-making to the future . . . it is their perennial proclamation to Heaven that beneath the broken wings of life they still retain a spiritual likeness to the God of all Goodness. And as such they command respect . . . it is important to lend them a helping hand. . . ." But a word of advice: *"If we showed more wit in avoiding temptation, we should find it easier to keep our . . . resolutions."* [214]

It is never wise to tempt temptation, to hover closely near the edge of a precipice, to see how far we can go without going too far. It is wiser, if possible, to separate ourselves from the associations or environment that tempt us to idleness or evil. A big part of the battle is in breaking the chain of events, in changing the routine that leads to temptation.

And "do not depend too blindly upon the supernatural. The devil is also supernatural . . . it is because we stay in the same old ruts so persistently that our own **particular** devil knows so well where to find us. . . . The thing to do is to change tactics. . . ."

Therefore, when temptation comes, "take a header somewhere . . . Use your imagination, think of something innocent and daring to do, and keep up your adventures till the astonished nerves and brain react and you forget in the novelty of new experiences the awful craving. Many a man would save himself . . . if he walked as far into the woods as his strength would carry him, or if . . . in such an emergency [he would talk to someone]. The important thing is to break the [chain]" [214]—to break the routine of temptation, to run, to walk, to talk, to think, to pray, to remove ourselves from the rut— from the very attitude and atmosphere of evil.

"If we showed more wit in avoiding temptation, we should find it easier to keep our . . . resolutions."

The Courage to Start—and to Stop

Three kinds of courage are required in all the shifting scenes—in all the trial and error, in all the learning and living of life: the courage to start, the courage to stop, and the courage to follow through.

Thoreau said: "I know of no more encouraging fact than the unquestionable ability of man to elevate his life by a conscious endeavor." [215] That conscious endeavor may be in the nature of starting in a new direction, of continuing in an old direction, or it may be in the nature simply of stopping something that never should have been started.

It is comforting to know that we *can* alter and elevate life by conscious endeavor. This implies a certain degree of flexibility, along with unchanging principles. We all go through some waste motion; we all make some mistakes; we all set out on some detours and pursue some wrong roads; and the dogged assumption (perhaps partly pride) that, once having started wrong, we have to follow through, is one reason why people sometimes find themselves in deep and dangerous ruts.

All the choices of life, all its habits, all the ruts, should be looked at forthrightly, searchingly, sincerely. Progress is a process of developing and doing —sometimes continuing, sometimes changing— pressing forward when we should, repenting when we should, and not feeling obliged to continue on any wrong road.

We should have the courage to start good things, to continue good things, to continue to learn, and to "hold fast that which is good." [216] We should also have the courage to stop, to leave behind a habit we should not have, no matter how tight its hold. In short, we need the courage to start and continue what we should do, and the courage to stop what we shouldn't do.

The First Mistake—and the Second

We have said elsewhere that "when we need repentance, we need it now." Sometimes, if we have made one mistake, we may think it will not matter much if we make one more of the same kind. We may fall into the fallacy of supposing that multiplying mistakes is not—additionally—so serious, when once a wrong direction has been taken.

This is, of course, an untenable position to take. It is certainly no *less* wrong—and may be much more—to make the second mistake than to make the first. The second false step is not more acceptable, not less serious, than the first. For the first we may plead innocence, or impetuousness, or ignorance—simply not knowing. For the second we can scarcely plead innocence or ignorance convincingly.

Stealing twice is surely not less serious than stealing once. A second act of immorality is certainly not less serious than the first. There is really no wholesale rate on sin or error or the making of mistakes—on the contrary, the more deliberate, the more experienced, the more intentional and frequent the offense, the more serious must be the mistakes.

And it is a gross fallacy to feel that, after one

mistake, another doesn't matter very much. Since life is everlasting, no matter how far we may have gone in a wrong direction it is always urgently important to get back to the right road. Only the right direction will get us out of wrong ways; the wrong direction never did. And just because a man may be down deep is no reason why he should go deeper.

Wherever one is, or has arrived, let him resolve to make his next move toward the right way, and not succumb to the false philosophy that following a first mistake by a second, or several, doesn't matter very much. It simply isn't so.

If You Shouldn't do It—Don't

Two sentences from popular plays suggest a subject: The first is the tearful outcry of a boy who has seen terrible tragedy result from a series of angry, senseless circumstances. "I wish," he says, "—I wish it was yesterday." [217]

The second is a similar wish, uttered by a woman who has pressed a point too far and has received an answer she would rather not have heard. "I wish it were five minutes ago," she says. [218]

"I wish it were yesterday." "I wish it were five minutes ago." "I wish I hadn't gone there." "I wish I hadn't done it." "I wish I hadn't said it."

We wish we had lived so that we would not have so much reason to wish we had done differently.

This is the looking back in life that too often makes us wish we had had greater foresight. Despite our best knowledge, our best judgment, and our best planning, there are accidents; and there are honest mistakes and miscalculations and unforeseen events that intervene. But there are also sometimes blind and stubborn mistakes, angry mistakes, or deliberately dishonest mistakes that ignore proved principles and morals and the keeping of commandments. And while we may not know exactly how we shall feel when we do something we know we

[179]

ought not to do, or say something we shouldn't say, we do know for a certainty that there will be uneasiness, anxiety, regret, or sorrow, and that we shall pay a penalty equal to or greater than any so-called satisfaction received.

We do know the principle of causes and consequences, and down deep within us we do have a warning, an inner awareness and resistance against any cheap or shoddy or dishonest or immoral or cruel or unkind act or utterance.

"I wish it were yesterday"—"I wish it were five minutes ago"—"I wish I hadn't said it"—"I wish I hadn't done it."

"Would you be exempt from uneasiness," said a time-respected source, "[then] do nothing you know or even suspect is wrong. Would you enjoy the purest pleasure; [then] do everything in your power which you [honestly] believe is right." [219]

And so we would plead with those who are young, and with others also: Avoid regret by standing up to standards.

If you shouldn't do it, don't.

"A Man Unconscious of His Faults"

It was said of a well-known person of the past, "Her vanity was too fundamental for her to profit by the stern lessons of experience. She could not face the fact that she was wrong, so she was unable to reform herself." [220]

This is a basic and penetrating theme: the admission of wrong, the willingness to face facts, to admit our own errors. What prevents it is sometimes pride, sometimes stubbornness, sometimes actual ignorance.

An eminent observer has this to say: "What progress can there be for a man unconscious of his faults? Such a man has lost the fundamental element of growth, which is the realization that there is something bigger, better, and more desirable than the condition in which he now finds himself. In the soil of self-satisfaction, true growth has poor nourishment. . . . Heaven pity the man who is unconscious of a fault! Pity him also who is ignorant of his ignorance!" [221]

Repentance, of course, is a great and indispensable principle—and yet repentance is impossible without the recognition of error, without admitting a mistake, without sincere searching of ourselves. So long as we rationalize and justify ourselves in wrongdoing, so long as we pamper our weaknesses and use the example of others who do wrong as a reason or excuse for ourselves, so long as we do not really reach for the improvement or perfection of which the Master spoke—so long as we surrender to our appetites and vanities, and justify and cover up our errors rather than seek to correct them—we shall not make much progress toward improvement.

"She could not face the fact that she was wrong, so she was unable to reform herself." "What progress can there be for a man unconscious of his faults?" As Carlyle commented: "The greatest of faults . . . is to be conscious of none." [4]

"... With One Step ..."

"The journey of a thousand miles begins with one step." [22] This ancient proverb applies to every side of life, to every decision, to our whole course of conduct and commitment: our choice of a profession or pursuit, our choice in making a marriage; to standards, thought, habit, and to every attitude and action.

This emphasizes the constant need for thoughtfulness in all things—for a respectful, prayerful approach to all problems. It reminds us also that there is no safety or assurance in a hasty, stubborn, shortsighted decision. Despite the tendency nowadays to ignore or explain away timeless standards and eternal truths, we live always with causes and consequences, and no amount of rationalizing can ever set them aside.

All experience in the past, and the happiness and heartaches of people living in the present, suggest the wisdom of a firm determination not to go one step on any wrong road. As to what should *not* be done, to youth and all the rest of us the proverb cited above says: Don't do it—don't even entertain the idea. To have the courage and conviction to say "No" is a great source of safety.

Life is always before us, the commandments are

always in force, and causes always lead to consequences. And we ought simply to decide what we should and shouldn't do, where we should and shouldn't go, and plant our feet firmly, not flirting with the questionable or unwholesome side of any situation.

Every step indicates a direction, and one step leads to the next unless there is some change—a reconsideration, a real repentance. But the safest course is not to need it. The next best is, when we need it, not to postpone repentance.

To realize the highest happiness, the peace and progress that a loving Father can give, we must remember that the journey of a thousand miles or years—indeed, of all eternity—begins with one step.

A Searching Appraisal

There are times for looking forward and times for looking back, and one is never wholly independent of the other—for what we become follows from what we have thought and been and done before. As we pause to appraise our actions and accomplishments, our acquisitions and attitudes, the summarizing of the past is sobering, yet the hope and promise of the future are before us.

In business, with good bookkeeping, we can tell with fair accuracy whether we have come out on the plus or minus side. In life this is not altogether easy. Our feelings and emotions are involved, our judgment and prejudices and various personal perspectives—all the human factors, all the intangibles. But we are not without standards in our self-appraisal—we are not without some means of measuring. While conscience may sometimes stretch to varying lengths of convenience, yet when a man sits down to an honest searching of himself he knows in some sense whether or not he is honest, whether he has represented facts fairly, whether he has cheated or overcharged, whether he has been clean, faithful, and honorable in thought and speech and act—whether in general he has tried to be his best or has withheld himself grudgingly from

[185]

full performance—whether he has honestly tried to keep the commandments. And if he has peace in his heart, the chances are that the answers to these questions will be fairly affirmative.

We have all made mistakes. Few of us are likely to be free of all regrets. For some, life may have been, as someone put it, "a succession of surrenders," with some things done and others left undone. But "let a man try faithfully, manfully to be right," said Carlyle, "and he will daily grow more and more right." [41]

A sincere, thoroughgoing appraisal is always in order, and blessedly there is in force the principle of repentance. Basically what is required is an honest attitude, an honest effort. Thank God that He has given us a time when, if we truly want to, we can in a sense—not for the past, but for the future— begin again, or at least begin to be what we ought to be.

* * *

"Come, my friends,
'Tis not too late to seek a newer world."
—Tennyson [222]

Courage, Fear, and Faith

"The future is no more uncertain than
the present."

—Walt Whitman [223]

Fear and Faith

In these times we see and hear and feel, almost from moment to moment, the heartbeat of the world and the impact of its problems, and earnestly we need the solid assurance of faith against fear. "Fear of misfortune," says an old proverb, "is worse than misfortune itself." [224]

The fact is that men are always subject to uncertainty. We all have troubles, fears, problems, and have to learn to live with them—or above them. This has always been so. Dr. John A. Widtsoe has said: "He who fears loses strength for the combat of life, for the fight against evil. Therefore, the power of evil ever seeks to engender fear in human hearts. . . . We must seek to dispel fear. . . . A timid, fearing people cannot do their work well. . . . [We] cannot afford to dissipate our strength in fear. . . . " [225]

In some meaningful sentences Robert Frost says: "In three words, I can sum up everything I've learned about life: It goes on. . . . The important thing to remember is that there is a direction and a continuity. . . . Despite our fears and worries . . . life continues. . . ." [25]

It does continue. And we have to meet it here and now, each day we live—and hereafter also.

There is no point in quaking with the impact of every hour. We have to have faith, the faith to quiet our hearts in the midst of confusion and uncertainties. We can't run away from everything; we can't keep on running from anything—for sooner or later we would run out of the strength to run. We have to live life, face it, honor it, enjoy it, adjust to it, in honest endeavor, doing what we can about what we don't like, and trusting to the future, with courage to be what we ought to be to the best of our ability.

To young men everywhere, to all others also: Have faith against fear, faith in the Father of us all, faith in the future, faith in freedom; faith with courage and conviction, pursuing solid plans and purposes, with an awareness of ultimate and timeless objectives. Despite the squalls and the storms, and even now and then soul-trying tempests, there is an overruling Providence. As we live to deserve His help, He will not forget us or leave us alone.

"One Step Enough for Me"

"Most of us," said an eminent American, "are living under a strain that human nature never was intended to bear." [226] All people have problems, and some days no doubt the difficulties and discouragements may seem almost unsurmountable. And being much preoccupied with our own problems, we are surprised sometimes to realize the problems and heartaches of others, and the burdens they have to bear. There is sorrow and disappointment in many hearts and homes. The fondest plans and hopes of many have had to be abandoned or long delayed. Most of us have had to reconcile ourselves to something less than we once wished for. We have had to readjust, to gather the threads together and save as much of the pattern as we can, and still carry on.

The old, the young, those in-between, all at times have their problems and perplexities. But our opportunity, our obligation, after all, is to do what we have to do a day at a time and not try to carry the whole future before us. Surely we cannot afford to be afraid of everything that ever could or might happen. This suggests a line from "Lead, Kindly Light": "I do not ask to see the distant scene. One step enough for me." [227]

We cannot see a hundred years or a hundred days or hours ahead, or even tomorrow morning. We must have patience and faith to take the first step we can see, and trust for the next step to show itself, and trust that the Light will ever lead us to meet each obligation and opportunity, knowing that there are plans and purposes and everlasting promise.

"Keep forever in view the momentous value of life." [228] "The best preparation for the future, is the present well seen to, and the last duty done." [229] "Let the peace of God rule in your hearts." [230] Move forward with faith. Be not afraid.

Courage against the Current

The world is complex. Life is complex. There are many demands upon us all, and we find ourselves needing to know more and more about *much more*, with less time for knowing all we need to know. With so many pressures and problems we are sometimes tempted to take the line of least resistance and hesitate to move contrary to the current.

Yet we have a real responsibility for our choices, our opinions, our principles—and we cannot safely assume that all things should be as they are. We cannot rightly excuse ourselves from the responsibility of seeing for ourselves where any trend or tendency, any drift or direction, is likely to take us. With freedom there is need of honest individualism, of frank thinking, of constructive suggestion. We have to have the courage to voice our honest views.

We should not be opposed to things because of stubbornness or pride, prejudice or perversity; neither should we assume that all is well without inquiring for ourselves. Where there is too much timidity, principles suffer, and so do people, and so does self-respect. We cannot safely isolate ourselves from issues. Nor should young people be content unthinkingly to follow the crowd. What "everyone is doing" is often a fleeting phase, a passing style that someone started. The crowd has no higher wisdom; it is made up of individuals, every one of whom should pause to consider, to think things through.

Criticism or opposition should never be petty, unreasoning or irresponsible. But we must have the courage to criticize constructively—to think, to speak, to be counted when occasion requires—to make our moral and honest individual force felt and never simply drift downstream with silent, unreasoning consent.

"What a new face courage puts on everything!" said Emerson.[231] To which another added, "Nothing but the right can ever be expedient." [44]

Courage—"a Passport to Respect"

Near the turn of the century, speaking before a
learned society, a statesman made these remarks: "The truth is that physical courage has
always been the most commonplace of virtues, . . .
so that it has become an unfailing proof of deca-
dence for any people to become hysterical over ex-
hibitions of animal courage without regard to moral
quality. . . . Just the contrary is true of moral courage. [It] is among the rarest of virtues, and its serv-
ices are of far greater value in the democratic ages
than ever before. Indeed, the day may not be distant when the existence of law and order . . . may
depend upon it. For that reason . . . the value of
courage in a government by the majority can hardly
be over-estimated . . . surely, if we are to find a bul-
wark of defense in our day of need, we ought to be
now commending it by our example, showing how
really brave men face grave problems . . . and set
themselves . . . to finding the best possible solutions
of them." [232]

There is a kind of courage which, Henry Ward
Beecher said, is the "passport to respect" [233]—the
"courage of the wise" as distinguished from the

"rash and foolish." [234] "True courage," said Paul Whitehead, "is not the brutal force of vulgar heroes, but the firm resolve of virtue and reason." [235] Those are significant words. *"The firm resolve of virtue and reason."*

Sooner or later in every person's life there are likely to be pressures and persuasions to compromise personal principles, and each man must make up his mind what he will do with his principles under pressure. If he forever compromises, forever gives ground, he may find in the end that he has run out of ground to give. Everyone has to stand with courage and conviction or lose respect, lose much of what makes him a man. "To see what is right and not do it," said Confucius, "is want of courage." [236] Scripture says on the subject: "Watch ye, stand fast in the faith, quit you like men." [237] "Be strong and of a good courage." [238]

Shakespeare said it unforgettably in a single short sentence: "Screw your courage to the sticking-place." [239] And he might have added, your principles and your convictions also.

To "a Skeptical World"

"No man adequate to do anything," said Carlyle, "but is first of all in right earnest about it; what I call a sincere man. I should say sincerity, a deep, great, genuine sincerity, is the first characteristic of all men in any way heroic. . . . He must have truth; truth which he feels to be true. How shall he stand otherwise? . . . Belief I define to be the healthy act of a man's mind. . . . Doubt, truly, is not itself a crime. Certainly we do not rush out, clutch up the first thing we find, and straightway believe that! All manner of . . . inquiry . . . about all manner of objects, dwells in every reasonable mind. . . . [But] truly it is a sad thing for a people, as for a man, to fall into skepticism, . . . into insincerity; . . . For this world, and for all worlds, what curse is so fatal? . . . For Skepticism is not intellectual only; it is moral also; a chronic atrophy and disease of the whole soul. . . . It seems to me, you lay your finger here on the heart of the world's maladies when you call it a Skeptical World. . . . It is out of this . . . that the whole tribe of social pestilences . . . have derived their being. . . . Do not sink yourselves in boundless bottomless abysses of Doubt, of wretched God-forgetting Unbelief . . . A man lives by believing something. . . ." [4]

[197]

So said Carlyle, and this we would add: The world, the universe, is a living, moving, ever present evidence of a Creator, an Intelligence beyond any or all of ours. Life cannot be explained away, nor can causes and consequences, nor all of nature's marvelous manifestations—nor man, nor his mind. "If a clock proves the existence of a clockmaker," said Voltaire, "and the world does not prove the existence of a Supreme Architect, then I consent to be called a fool." [240] To certain learned Frenchmen who had proved "by all manner of logic that there could not be a God, Napoleon, looking up at the stars, remarked, "Very ingenious, Messieurs; but *who made* all that?" [4]

With all this before us, God grant us the blessing of believing, for the world does exist, and so does the universe, and so do we, and so do our loved ones, and life itself. This is no whim or delusion— and the reality of all this is reason enough for humility, for goodness, for reverence, for respect; for living earnestly, preparing ourselves fully, for keeping the commandments, and for holding to faith in the future.

* * *

"Epochs of faith are epochs of fruitfulness; but epochs of unbelief are barren."

—Goethe [241]

"There Is No Wealth but Life"

"Life is eternal; and love is immortal;
   and death is only a horizon;
 and a horizon is nothing save the limit of
   our sight."
                     —Rossiter Worthington Raymond [242]

There Is No Wealth, but Life

"It's Life That Matters"

From Dostoevsky comes the poignant comment of a young man who knew he had little left of mortal life. "It's natural to believe," he says, "that everyone else thinks too little of life and is apt to waste it too cheaply, and to use it too lazily, too shamelessly. . . . It's life that matters, nothing but life—the process of discovering, the everlasting and perpetual process. . . . If he's alive he has everything in his power! Whose fault is it he doesn't understand that?" [125]

"If he's alive he has everything!" Without life we have nothing. And he who has only mortal life, only limited life, has too little, since every day brings him nearer to the end of all that has meaning for him. It is as Ruskin remarked—"There is no wealth but life." [243] Therefore the impact of this passage: "Behold, He that hath eternal life is rich." [244]

This brings us again to the importance of belief, the importance of perspective, the importance of putting important and unimportant things in their proper place—for what we believe about ourselves, about others, about God, about life, is of incalculable consequence, since what a man believes or knows or thinks he is, and what he thinks life's purpose is, largely determine how he lives; and how he lives largely determines what he is like—including the accumulations that represent his efforts and interests.

Not to work for what we believe would be a waste of life. And we would do well to look to what we do, to what we make; to what causes we serve, to all our choices, and to the commandments we keep; to the love and respect of family and friends, and to the reality of our relationship to Him who made us in His image, and from whom we have the assurance that people and personality are eternal and that hereafter, even as here, we shall know and recognize, in literal reality, our family and friends—and shall always be our separate selves.

Time is short—but eternity is endlessly long. "It's life that matters . . . the everlasting perpetual process." He who is alive has everything—"Whose fault is it if he doesn't understand that?"

"What Have We Got to Lose?"

Often we hear people discuss the odds on certain prospects or proposals—the chances of winning or losing, of success or failure in various matters. And sometimes we hear quite casually the question, "What have we got to lose?"

There are many hazards in life, many chances, many so-called "calculated risks." But the hazards and the risks can be reduced by the sincere resolve not to take dishonest or unethical or illegal chances —not to run against the law, the commandments, the rules of health, the rules of safety, or the time-proved principles.

Arthur Brisbane once said: "Life is a short walk along a narrow thread . . . beginning and ending in a mysterious unknown. . . . Life is short as we see it, but in reality . . . never ends—and, long or short, it is all that we have." [245] Life *is* all we have, here or hereafter. And since this is so, no one can wisely takes chances in matters of morals, or honesty, or other things incompatible with a quiet conscience. As to lawlessness or any evil action, even if we don't get caught by someone else, we get caught by our

[203]

own conscience—caught with loss of self-respect, with not liking ourselves inside.

The odds on losing health, on losing honor, on losing life or loved ones, or losing a quiet conscience, can scarcely be considered a good gamble. And to anyone who says you probably won't get hurt, or probably won't get caught, or most likely will get away with it, the wise answer would be: "I am not interested in the odds or the averages—I am all I have. Life is all I have."

The odds and the averages are not much comfort to someone who loses what is personally most precious and important to him. Anyone who takes a dare he should not take, or involves himself in shady ventures, or gambles his health, his happiness, his peace, his principles—anyone who takes a so-called calculated risk where such precious and irreplaceable things are laid on the line—would prove himself almost incredibly unwise, no matter what he thinks the odds are.

In all such situations the answer could be simply: "I'm not interested in the odds. I am all I have —life is all I have—life and loved ones everlastingly."

What do we have to lose? In the words of Albert Camus: "We have nothing to lose—except everything." [246]

"A Calm, Unshakable Faith"

Two statements on the immortality of man appeared in print about half a century ago, which we recall:

"If we neglect the divine . . . and give ourselves over wholly to the human . . . we may certainly count upon nothing but a triumph of pessimism. For . . . no matter how bravely the body fights, the years inevitably overcome it, bow it, break it . . . [and] at last, true optimism must rest upon a calm, unshakable faith in eternal life and in the unlimited goodness of him who gives it. Short of such faith . . . when worldly sources fail one by one . . . there is no escaping hopeless pessimism. . . . Blessed is [he] who walks in the light of divine faith." [247]

And the other: "We rest on no new reason for believing in the immortality of the soul. The old reasons . . . are quite sufficient . . . although we welcome the search. As yet the instinctive longing of the soul for its own immortality, and the testimony of the resurrection of Jesus Christ, are our sufficient ground of belief. . . . If we have reason to believe that there is a Divine Spirit, it is easy to believe that there are other subordinate spirits, human spirits, and that these spirits of ours may survive the body. So all religious faith and all hope of immortality begins with God, and rests on Him. We came from him; we go to him. He lives, we live. . . . Why should not a Father reveal himself to his children. Why should he not send prophets and teachers, and why not a supreme Teacher, a Son of God and a Son of Man? . . . Why should he not bring us a word from God, and why should he not assure us of immortality by his own resurrection? . . . How can a man assert that nothing but matter exists, that there is no such thing as an immaterial soul? . . . What right has he to claim that there is only one kind of existence, and that material? . . . we rest on the fact of One who died and rose from the dead, whose name we give to our faith, and whose triumph over death is our triumph also." [248]

An intelligent Creator would not give us the power to learn just to let that learning be lost; would not let life and loved ones become dear just to let that dearness disappear in death. When all of life and all the endless future lie before us, it is no time to let half-doubts keep us from living, from preparing, from enjoying the long journey of everlasting life. We witness here that Jesus is the Christ, the Son of God, who died and lived again, and did redeem us from death.

As to Ultimate Answers . . .

These are days when men are earnestly searching for answers. So perplexing are the problems that superficial answers will not satisfy—for it
is more than a matter of temporal or surface considerations. It comes down to a question of what
men really are, what they should be, where they
came from, where they are going, and why they
are here.

Is time all there is? Is there eternity beyond time?
Is personality perpetuated? Can we count on the
love and companionship of loved ones beyond the
limits of this life? Will we hereafter really recognize family and friends? Are men immortal in the
literal, substantive sense—or is immortality only a
manner of speaking, such as living in our descend-
ants, or such as our service or influence that is
forever felt?

And why are such questions important? Why
can we not live life as it comes, from day to day,
and cease concerning ourselves about ultimate answers?

One reason is because what we are—or think we
are—largely determines how we live, what we do
with life. He who thinks there is no immortality,
no accountability, no continuance—no heaven or

hereafter—is likely to live a different life from him who believes in a literal and loving eternal Father, who sent us here and expects us to return to account for what we have done with the opportunities we have had. What men think they are, what they believe about life and its length, its purpose, its ultimate objectives, separates them in many essentials.

Now, as to a conviction concerning things we can count on, including our conviction concerning Jesus the Christ—that He did live, die, and rise again on the third day; that He did break the bonds of death and assure us all everlasting life—God has not deceived us in this assurance. He who keeps the stars in their courses has given us this that we can count on. This was the mission and message of the Master, of the Savior and Redeemer of mankind. This was the cause for His coming.

And we witness this day His divinity and the literal reality of His resurrection, as with our loved ones we move on to a personal everlasting life, toward the answers and the peace we so much seek, and with a conviction we cannot deny. As Job said it, in these wonderful words: "I know that my redeemer liveth." [206]

"And This, Too, Shall Pass"

More than a century ago, Abraham Lincoln recounted a legend that suggests a searching of our pursuits, our surroundings, ourselves. A certain monarch, he said, "once ordered his wise men to invent him a sentence . . . which should be true and appropriate in all times and situations. They presented him the words, 'And this, too, shall pass away.' . . . How much it expresses! How chastening in the hour of pride! How consoling in the depths of affliction! 'And this, too, shall pass away.' And yet, let us hope, it is quite not true. Let us hope, rather, that by the best cultivation of the physical world . . . around us, and the intellectual and moral world within us, we shall secure [that] which . . . shall not pass away." [249]

Some things pass. Some things endure. Sorrows and disappointments pass. So do long periods of preparation. In our minds we may place limits on how long we can put up with certain situations or difficulties. But if we can endure one hour, one day, we usually find we can continue. No man knows how much he can endure until he must. Strength and patience and ability increase with necessity.

Certain things sometimes seem exceedingly important—things we have set our hearts on and feel

we must have—yet time passes, and what once com-
pelled us, does so less urgently. Fashions pass. Success passes; and so, frequently, does failure. The
struggle, the running pace, the grasping, the getting, and the gathering, the exhausting effort to
keep up with others—these pass. The hurts and
heartbreaks, the pain—these pass. Friends pass,
loved ones; youth passes into age, and both into
eternity.

But what must not, cannot pass, is life's great
purpose, the reason that the universe and men
were made; and faith in God our Father, in our
relationship to Him, in His reality and reachability;
in His unfailing interest in us always—these do not
pass. Nor does the peace that finally comes with
faith, with sanity of values, with a quiet conscience,
with knowing a goodness that *is* its own reward,
and knowing that limitlessly beyond are life and
loved ones, and an eternity of all that deeply matters most.

These do not pass.

"... Work a Little Longer ...
Then Follow ..."

From Carlyle we quote these lines on the loss of the most beloved companion of his life—the wife of whom he wrote in reminiscence:

"Strange how she made the desert blossom for herself and me . . . what a palace she . . . made of that wild moorland home of the poor man! . . . She was my angel and unwearied helper and comforter. . . . Oh, . . . be wise, all ye living, and remember that time passes. . . . Fools, fools! we forget that it has to end; so this has ended. . . ." [56]

This is the anguished utterance of many who, like Carlyle, have lost those they love: "so this has ended"—and the longer we live the more aware we are of the shortness of this life we live, and ever in the background are the questions that confront us as those whom we have loved leave us one by one: Where are they? What lies beyond? Shall we know them as we knew them here? Is life indeed everlasting?

Thank God for the assurance that it is and shall be so, and for the fullness of the faith that we shall know and see again, to love, to live with those whom we have loved and lost. Such assurance comes from Him who gave us life, from whom we have the miracle of birth, the miracle of spring's return, as trees once dormant break forth one day into full flower—a miracle which in some respects has come to seem quite commonplace, but which is part of all the evidence and answer of the miracle—and yet reality—of everlasting life.

And the softening touch of this assurance seemed to come to Carlyle's awareness as he left these further lines: "Sometimes [there is] the image of her, . . . as if nodding to me with a smile, 'I am gone, loved one; work a little longer, . . . [then] . . . follow. There is no baseness, and no misery here.' . . . Blind and deaf that we are; oh, think, if thou yet love anybody living, wait not till death sweeps down the paltry little dust-clouds and idle dissonances of the moment. . . ." [56]

Thank God for blessed memories of those who once were with us—and for the real and literal assurance of everlasting life that makes memories more meaningful—that makes memories but the promise of the unfulfilled future.

* * *

"Spend your time in nothing which you know must be repented of; in nothing on which you might not pray for the blessing of God; in nothing which you could not review with a quiet conscience on your dying bed; in nothing which you might not safely and properly be found doing if death should surprise you in the act."

—Richard Baxter [122]

Index of References to Quoted Passages

40. Editorial, *The Outlook,* Apr. 8, 1905, 48
41. Thomas Carlyle, 49, 69, 186
42. Lydia H. Sigourney (1791-1865), Am. auth., 50
43. John Fiske (1842-1901), Am. auth., 50
44. Richard Whately (1787-1863), Eng. clergy, 50, 194
45. Edwin Hubbell Chapin (1814-80), Am. Unit. clergy, 51
46. Tryon Edwards (1809-94), Am. theol. and editor, 52
47. Nathaniel Emmons (1745-1840), Am. theol., 52
48. Edward Young (1683-1765), Eng. poet, 52
49. To Dwight Whitney Morrow by Anne Morrow Lindbergh, 53
50. Cyril Northcote Parkinson, 53
51. Sir Matthew Hale (1790-1879), Eng. jurist, 54
52. Robert G. Ingersoll, *About Farming in Illinois,* 54
53. Emerson, *Conduct of Life: Wealth,* 54
54. Henrik Ibsen, *A Doll's House,* Act I, 54
55. Frances Starr, *My Views on Marriage,* 55
56. Thomas Carlyle, *Reminiscences,* 58, 88, 90, 91, 211, 212
57. St. Francis de Sales (1567-1622), French bishop, 59
58. Francis de S. Fenelon (1651-1715), French archbishop, 64
59. John Tillotson (1630-94), Archbishop of Canterbury, 65
60. Richard Cecil (1748-77), Eng. divine, 65
61. Shakespeare, *Hamlet,* Act III, 65
62. "Cain's Hundred," MGM-NBC TV film series, 65
63. William Penn, *Some Fruits of Solitude,* 67, 70
64. Cicero, *On Friendship,* 67

65. Emerson, *Man the Reformer,* 68
66. Doctrine and Covenants 42:45, 68, 70
67. New Testament, John 15:12, 68
68. Charles Simmons (1798-1856), Am. clergy, 69
69. Owen D. Young, Am. law. and financier, 69
70. Arthur P. Stanley (1815-81), Eng. clergy, 69
71. George Eliot (1819-80), Eng. novelist, 69, 79, 95, 110
72. Book of Mormon, Mosiah 4:11-16, 69, 70
73. Author unknown, 70, 83
74. George Herbert (1593-1633), Eng. philos., 71
75. Doctrine and Covenants 58:43, 74
76. New Testament, John 8:11, 74
77. George R. Means, Gen. Secretary's Letter to Rotary International officials, July 27, 1962, 74
78. Goethe, *Elective Affinities,* bk. 1, 74
79. Caroline Atherton Briggs Mason, *Do They Miss Me At Home?,* 75
80. Edmund Vance Cooke (1866-1932), Am. auth. and lec., 84
81. William Goldsmith Brown, *Mother, Home, Heaven,* 85
82. Jean Ingelow, *Songs of Seven: Seven Times Six,* 85
83. Mary Stewart Cutting, *What Is a Successful Husband?,* 86
84. Temple Bailey, *A Little Parable for Mother,* 86
85. To Nathaniel Babson by Roger W. Babson, 87, 88
86. To John Wallace Hamilton by John Wallace Hamilton Jr., 89
87. To John D. Rockefeller, Jr. by Abby Aldrich Rockefeller, 90

137. Piotr Tchaikovsky, July 6, 1878, 127
138. New Testament, Matt. 7:7, 128
139. Doctrine and Covenants 58:27, 128, 136
140. Reported by Rebecca West (1892-), Scot. novelist, 129
141. Giuseppe Mazzini (1805-72), It. patriot, 129
142. Karl Wilhelm Humboldt (1767-1835), Ger. states., 130
143. Calvin Coolidge, 130
144. Robin G. Collingwood (1889-1943), Eng. philos. and hist., 130
145. John Jay (1745-1829), Ch. Jus. U.S. Sup. Court, 130
146. Adam Clarke (1762-1832), Eng. divine, 130
147. George B. Cortelyou (1862-1940), U.S. Cabinet officer, 130
148. William Ellery Channing, *Elevation of the Laboring Classes,* 131
149. James Parton, (1822-91), Am. biographer, 131
150. Robert Browning, *In a Balcony,* 132
151. Henry Ward Beecher (1813-87), Am. clergy, 143
152. Charles Reade (1814-84), Eng. novelist, 134
153. Editorial, *The Independent,* Aug. 1898, 135
154. Plato, 136
155. Old Testament, Eccles. 11:1, 138
156. New Testament, see Mark 8:35, 138
157. Julia Louise Matilda Woodruff, *Gone,* 138
158. Rudyard Kipling, *For All We Have and Are,* 139
159. Carl Lotus Becker (1873-1945), Am. historian, 141
160. John Foster Dulles, 141, 142
161. Patrick Henry, 142

162. Seneca (4 B.C.-65 A.D.), Roman Stoic philos., 142, 143, 144
163. Woodrow Wilson, speech, New York Press Club, Sept. 9, 1912, 142
164. Charles Sumner, Senator, *Oration on the True Grandeur of Nations,* Boston, July 4, 1845, 142, 148
165. James Madison, 143
166. Edmund Burke (1729-97), Eng. states., 143
167. Theodore Roosevelt, speech delivered at Chicago, Apr. 10, 1899, titled *On National Questions,* 143, 144
168. Kahlil Gibran, *The Prophet,* 145, 146
169. Robert Dunning Dripps, *The Constitution of the American Citizen Unafraid,* 146
170. Matthew Hale Carpenter, *Mission and Future Policy of the United States,* 146
171. Joseph Smith, *The Principle of Religion,* 146
172. Doctrine and Covenants, 101:80, 146
173. James Madison, *The Federalist* No. 51, Feb. 8, 1788, 147, 149
174. Judge Learned Hand, 148
175. George Washington to Marquis de Lafayette, May 28, 1788, 148
176. William Maxwell Evarts, *What the Age Owes to America,* from Centennial oration delivered at Philadelphia, July 4, 1876, 148
177. Book of Mormon, II Nephi, 10:10-14, 148, 154
178. Benjamin Franklin to David Hartley, Dec. 4, 1789, 148
179. Benjamin Franklin, excerpt from speech before the Constitutional Convention, 149
180. Ira Jewell Williams, *The Way of Safety for America,* 1923, 150

181. Dean Russell (pamphlet on *The Bill of Rights*), 150
182. Jim Bishop, *The Day Lincoln Was Shot*, 151
183. Lincoln-Douglas Debates, 151
184. Lincoln, address on *Colonization to a Deputation of Colored Men*, Aug. 14, 1862, 151, 152
185. *Ibid.*, letter to Maj.-Gen. Joseph Hooker, Jan. 26, 1863, 152
186. *Ibid.*, excerpts from Proclamation, Mar. 30, 1863, 152
187. *Ibid.*, Gettysburg Address, 152
188. Edward Everett, address, Charlestown, Mass., July 4, 1828, 153
189. David E. Lilienthal, *This I Do Believe*, 153
190. Andrew Jackson, *Farewell Address*, 154
191. W. Somerset Maugham, *Strictly Personal*, 154
192. Attributed to James C. Penney (also other sources), 154
193. Samuel Francis Smith, *America*, 154
194. Editorial, *The Independent*, Oct. 6, 1898, 157
195. Aesop, 157
196. Abraham Lincoln, Proclamation of Thanksgiving, Oct. 3, 1863, 158
197. Editorial, *The Outlook*, Nov. 29, 1902, 159, 161, 162
198. *Ibid.*, Nov. 26, 1904, 160, 161, 163
199. New Testament, Matt. 25:34-40, 164
200. Edgar A. Guest, 165
201. New Testament, I Pet. 1:22, 165
202. See New Testament, Matt. 19:19, 165
203. Old Testament, Deut. 10:19, 165
204. See New Testament, Luke 6:27, 165
205. *Ibid.*, Matt. 22:37, 165
206. Old Testament, Job 19:25, 166, 208
207. Susan Coolidge, 167
208. Robert Millikan, 168
209. Milton, *Paradise Lost*, 168
210. Doctrine and Covenants, 88:47, 168
211. Thomas Chalmers (1780-1847), Scot. divine, 168
212. Nietzsche, *Ecce Homo*, 169
213. Editorial, *The Independent*, Jan. 9, 1908, 171, 172
214. *Ibid.*, Jan. 7, 1903, 173, 174
215. Henry David Thoreau, 175
216. New Testament, I Thess. 5:21, 176
217. *West Side Story*, 179
218. "Checkmate" (*The Star System*), 179
219. Rules of Life, published in *The New Dictionary of Thoughts*, 180
220. David Cecil, *Melbourne*, 181
221. David O. McKay, *Gospel Ideals*, 181
222. Tennyson, *Ulysses*, 186
223. Walt Whitman, *The Broad-Ax*, 187
224. Cited by Najile S. Khoury, 189
225. Dr. John A. Widtsoe, 189
226. Harry Emerson Fosdick, *Twelve Tests of Character*, 191
227. John Henry Newman, *Lead, Kindly Light*, 191
228. John Foster (1836-1917), Am. lawyer, 192
229. George Macdonald (1824-1905), Scot. novelist, 192
230. New Testament, Col. 3:15, 192
231. Emerson, *Letters and Social Aims*, 194
232. Wayne Macveagh, *Ideals in American Politics*, 1901, 195
233. Henry Ward Beecher, *At the Raising of "The Old Flag,"* 1865, 195
234. William Jones, of Nayland, (1726-1800), 195, 196

Index of Subjects

[218]

[219]

[220]

89, 118; health, 120; work, 129, 130; peace, 184 (*see* Conscience)

HAVE FAITH IN THE FUTURE, 11

HEALTH, 28, 37, 113-123, 160, 201-203

HEAVEN, 78, 85, 207 (*see* Children)

HERITAGE, clean, for children, 90; of freedom, 146, 148, 151

HEROES BEHIND THE SCENES, 133

HOME, and debt, 54; and family circle, 77, 78; sweet sound of, 85 (*see* Children)

HONESTY, 21, 98

HONOR, man of, 16

HOW TO LIVE WITH UNCERTAINTY, 15

HUMILITY, 50, 108, 157, 161, 198

HUMOR, and trivialities, 41, 42; and marriage, 60

IDLENESS, 16 (*see* Work)

IF YOU SHOULDN'T DO IT—DON'T! 179

IGNORING, what we know, 28

IGNORANCE, voluntary, 25, 26; impossible to be saved in, 27; and knowledge, 27; in action, 27; untruth of, 99; knowingly, 106; pleading, 177; ignorant of, 181

IMMORALITY, and ideals, 74

IMMORTALITY, of families, 87-90; and loss of loved ones, 87-92, 160, 205-212; personal, 202, 207, 208; and faith, 205, 206; of the soul, 205, 206 (*see* Children)

IMPERFECTIONS, all have, 64

IMPRESSIONS, importance of, 77; wrong, 105, 106

IMPROVE(MENT), 33, 34, 128, 172, 181, 182 (*see* Repentance)

INDULGENCE, 23, 24, 27, 28, 37, 45, 46, 50, 67, 119, 120 (*see* Self-Control)

INFLUENCE, all have, 44; and solvency, 54; accountable for, 51

"INNOCENCE" OF INTENT, 103

INSIGNIFICANT, eliminating the, 113, 114

INSINCERITY, 12 (*see* Sincerity)

INSPIRATION, waiting for, 127

INSTITUTION(AL) and personal responsibility, 51, 52; cannot take place of parents, 82

INTEGRITY, in work, 132

INTELLIGENCE, glory of God is, 26

INTERRUPTIONS, in life, 15, 16, 135, 136

"IS NOT THE TRUTH THE TRUTH?" 99

"IT'S LIFE THAT MATTERS," 201

JESUS THE CHRIST (*see also* God), and truth, 99; birth of, 166; divinity of, 166, 206, 208; and perfection, 182; resurrection of, 166, 205-208

JOY, man is that he might have, 39, 46

JUDGING, by one foolish utterance, 33

JUDGMENTS, of God will be fair, 44

JULY FOURTH, 139-153

JUSTIFYING, ourselves, 43, 44, 181, 182

KINDNESS, in marriage, 57-73; family, 75-91; speech, 93-109

KNOWING IS NOT ENOUGH, 27

KNOWING, truth, 25, 26

KNOWLEDGE, is power, 27; and ignorance, 27; must be lived by, 28; acquiring, 31

LAW, gratitude for, 147; respect for, 150 (*see* God)

LAZINESS, and success, 30, 127 (*see* Work)

LEARN(ING) process of, 15-17, 27, 30, 33; cannot, for others, 138; privilege of, 163

"LET THE NATION SEARCH ITSELF," 161

LIBERTY, and conscience, 37; no, if we forget God, 141; to obey God is, 142 (*see* Freedom)

LIES, and half-truths, 97-102 (*see* Truth)

LIFE, and preparation, 11, 12, 15; increasing speed of, 17, 18; disciplined, 18; value of, 20, 157, 192, 201-211; passing of, 23, 87, 113, 183, 189; and learning, 34, 108, 158; simple and straight, 37, 38; degrading by follies, 37; everlasting, 38, 199, 201, 203; balanced, 89, 113-123; purpose in, 114; let man's, be true, 132; and heroism, 133, 134; stretching, 138; gratitude for, 160; is complex, 193, 194; cannot be explained away, 198; all we have, 203; from day to day, 207, 211, 212 (*see* Immortality)

LIKE PRACTICING IN PUBLIC, 33

LINCOLN, 151, 152, 158